JEAN-FRANÇOIS LYOTARD

'An excellent introduction to Lyotard's contribution to contemporary thought. It is lucid, to the point and persuasive.'

Hans Bertens, *University of Utrecht*

'This is a clear and concise introduction to all the major aspects of Lyotard's thought, which demonstrates just why this figure has had such a profound impact on contemporary life.'

Stuart Sim, *University of Sunderland*

In works such as *The Postmodern Condition, The Differend, Libidinal Economy* and *The Inhuman*, Jean-François Lyotard has radically transformed the ways in which we think about contemporary culture. His studies of the relations between knowledge, art, politics and history constitute some of the most influential texts in what has come to be known as postmodernist thought.

This guide offers an introduction to the key ideas which run through Lyotard's work, from modernity and the postmodern to ethics, the sublime and the 'unpresentable'. Simon Malpas places the key texts in their intellectual contexts and goes on to trace their considerable impact upon contemporary thought. In this way, he not only makes Lyotard's texts approachable, but also prepares readers to make their own critical judgements of the works. The book concludes with an annotated guide to further reading, with helpful suggestions for further study.

Lyotard's work is impossible to ignore for anybody who is serious about contemporary literature and culture, and this guide provides the ideal companion to the wide variety of his critical texts.

Simon Malpas is Lecturer in English at Manchester Metropolitan University. He is editor of *Postmodern Debates* and co-editor of *The New Aestheticism*.

ROUTLEDGE CRITICAL THINKERS
essential guides for literary studies

Series Editor: Robert Eaglestone, Royal Holloway, University of London

Routledge Critical Thinkers is a series of accessible introductions to key figures in contemporary critical thought.

With a unique focus on historical and intellectual contexts, each volume examines a key theorist's:

- significance
- motivation
- key ideas and their sources
- impact on other thinkers

Concluding with extensively annotated guides to further reading, *Routledge Critical Thinkers* are the literature student's passport to today's most exciting critical thought.

Already available:
Jean Baudrillard by Richard J. Lane
Maurice Blanchot by Ullrich Haase and William Large
Judith Butler by Sara Salih
Gilles Deleuze by Claire Colebrook
Sigmund Freud by Pamela Thurschwell
Martin Heidegger by Timothy Clark
Fredric Jameson by Adam Roberts
Paul de Man by Martin McQuillan
Edward Said by Bill Ashcroft and Pal Ahluwalia
Gayatri Chakravorty Spivak by Stephen Morton

For further details on this series,
see www.literature.routledge.com/rct

JEAN-FRANÇOIS LYOTARD

Simon Malpas

Routledge
Taylor & Francis Group

LONDON AND NEW YORK

First published 2003
by Routledge
11 New Fetter Lane, London EC4P 4EE

Simultaneously published in the USA and Canada
by Routledge
29 West 35th Street, New York, NY 10001

Routledge is an imprint of the Taylor & Francis Group

Typeset in Perpetua by
Florence Production Ltd, Stoodleigh, Devon
Printed and bound in Great Britain by
Biddles Ltd, Guildford and King's Lynn

British Library Cataloguing in Publication Data
A catalogue record for this book is available from the British Library

Library of Congress Cataloging in Publication Data
Malpas, Simon.
  Jean-François Lyotard/Simon Malpas.
    p. cm.—(Routledge critical thinkers)
  Includes bibliographical references and index.
  1. Lyotard, Jean François. I. Title. II. Series.
  B2430.L964 M25 2002   2002068187
  194–dc21

ISBN 0–415–25614–3 (hbk)
ISBN 0–415–25615–1 (pbk)

CONTENTS

SERIES EDITOR'S PREFACE

The books in this series offer introductions to major critical thinkers who have influenced literary studies and the humanities. The *Routledge Critical Thinkers* series provides the books you can turn to first when a new name or concept appears in your studies.

Each book will equip you to approach a key thinker's original texts by explaining her or his key ideas, putting them into context and, perhaps most importantly, showing you why this thinker is considered to be significant. The emphasis is on concise, clearly written guides which do not presuppose a specialist knowledge. Although the focus is on particular figures, the series stresses that no critical thinker ever existed in a vacuum but, instead, emerged from a broader intellectual, cultural and social history. Finally, these books will act as a bridge between you and the thinker's original texts: not replacing them but rather complementing what she or he wrote.

These books are necessary for a number of reasons. In his 1997 autobiography, *Not Entitled*, the literary critic Frank Kermode wrote of a time in the 1960s:

> On beautiful summer lawns, young people lay together all night, re-
> covering from their daytime exertions and listening to a troupe of
> Balinese musicians. Under their blankets or their sleeping bags, they
> would chat drowsily about the gurus of the time. . . . What they repeated
> was largely hearsay; hence my lunchtime suggestion, quite impromptu,
> for a series of short, very cheap books offering authoritative but intelli-
> gible introductions to such figures.

There is still a need for 'authoritative and intelligible introductions'. But this series reflects a different world from the 1960s. New thinkers have emerged and the reputations of others have risen and fallen, as new research has developed. New methodologies and challenging ideas have spread through the arts and humanities. The study of literature is no longer – if it ever was – simply the study and evalua- tion of poems, novels and plays. It is also the study of the ideas, issues and difficulties which arise in any literary text and in its interpretation. Other arts and humanities subjects have changed in analogous ways.

With these changes, new problems have emerged. The ideas and issues behind these radical changes in the humanities are often presented without reference to wider contexts or as theories which you can simply 'add on' to the texts you read. Certainly, there's nothing wrong with picking out selected ideas or using what comes to hand – indeed, some thinkers have argued that this is, in fact, all we can do. However, it is sometimes forgotten that each new idea comes from the pattern and development of somebody's thought and it is important to study the range and context of their ideas. Against theories 'floating in space', the *Routledge Critical Thinkers* series places key thinkers and their ideas firmly back in their contexts.

More than this, these books reflect the need to go back to the thinker's own texts and ideas. Every interpretation of an idea, even the most seemingly innocent one, offers its own 'spin', implicitly or explicitly. To read only books on a thinker, rather than texts by that thinker, is to deny yourself a chance of making up your own mind.

Sometimes what makes a significant figure's work hard to approach is not so much its style or content as the feeling of not knowing where to start. The purpose of these books is to give you a 'way in' by offering an accessible overview of a these thinkers' ideas and works and by guiding your further reading, starting with each thinker's own texts. To use a metaphor from the philosopher Ludwig Wittgenstein (1889–1951), these books are ladders, to be thrown away after you have climbed to the next level. Not only, then, do they equip you to approach new ideas, but also they empower you, by leading you back to a theorist's own texts and encouraging you to develop your own informed opinions.

Finally, these books are necessary because, just as intellectual needs have changed, the education systems around the world – the contexts in which introductory books are usually read – have changed radically, too. What was suitable for the minority higher education system of the 1960s is not suitable for the larger, wider, more diverse, high technology education systems of the twenty-first century. These changes call not just for new, up-to-date, introductions but new methods of presentation. The presentational aspects of *Routledge Critical Thinkers* have been developed with today's students in mind.

Each book in the series has a similar structure. They begin with a section offering an overview of the life and ideas of each thinker and explain why she or he is important. The central section of each book discusses the thinker's key ideas, their context, evolution and reception. Each book concludes with a survey of the thinker's impact, outlining how their ideas have been taken up and developed by others. In addition, there is a detailed final section suggesting and describing books for further reading. This is not a 'tacked-on' section but an integral part of each volume. In the first part of this section you will find brief descriptions of the thinker's key works, then, following this, information on the most useful critical works and, in some cases, on relevant web sites. This section will guide you in your reading, enabling you to follow your interests and develop your own projects. Throughout each book, references are given in what is known as the Harvard system (the author and the date of a work cited are given in the text and you can look up the full details in the bibliography at the back). This offers a lot of information in very little space. The books also explain technical terms and use boxes to describe events or ideas in more detail, away from the main emphasis of the discussion. Boxes are also used at times to highlight definitions of terms frequently used or coined by a thinker. In this way, the boxes serve as a kind of glossary, easily identified when flicking through the book.

The thinkers in the series are 'critical' for three reasons. First, they are examined in the light of subjects which involve criticism: principally literary studies or English and cultural studies, but also other disciplines which rely on the criticism of books, ideas, theories and unquestioned assumptions. Second, studying their work will provide you with a 'tool kit' for informed critical reading and thought, which will heighten your own criticism. Third, these thinkers are critical because they are crucially important: they deal with ideas and questions which can overturn conventional understandings of the world, of texts, of everything we take for granted, leaving us with a deeper understanding of what we already knew and with new ideas.

No introduction can tell you everything. However, by offering a way into critical thinking, this series hopes to begin to engage you in an activity which is productive, constructive and potentially life-changing.

ACKNOWLEDGEMENTS

I should like to thank the following people for their extremely helpful contributions to the writing of this book: Bob Eaglestone and Liz Thompson who have been exemplary editors, offering encouragement, support and acute advice throughout the writing process; the readers for Routledge (Hans Bertens, Richard Lane and Stuart Sim) who provided sensitive and constructive criticism of the first draft; my colleagues and students in the English and Philosophy Departments at Manchester Metropolitan University, particularly Barry Atkins, Kate McGowan and Jo Smith who spent time discussing ideas with me; and Erikka Askeland who read more drafts of the manuscript than she could possibly have been interested by.

WHY LYOTARD?

Jean-François Lyotard (1925–98) was one of the foremost critical thinkers of the second half of the twentieth century. He is most famous for his groundbreaking analyses of postmodernism and postmodernity, which will form the main focus of this book and will be introduced fully later on. These came into focus in his 1979 book, *The Postmodern Condition: A Report on Knowledge*, which has been widely discussed by critics and is often set as a key text on degree courses in English, Cultural and Media Studies, Philosophy and Sociology. Lyotard's book is one of the founding texts of postmodern theory, and has remained influential since its first publication. In a brilliant series of short chapters he analyses the controls placed on knowledge and power by governments, corporations and the international markets. This book will be the subject of Chapter 1 of the Key Ideas section. However, as well as *The Postmodern Condition*, his many other works written during a long career also demonstrate a wide-ranging set of interests in culture, politics and art, and raise challenging questions for anybody working in the Humanities today. The aim of this book is to introduce readers to some of Lyotard's most important critical analyses of the contemporary world, and to begin to explain his postmodern philosophy.

Questions about politics, justice and freedom lie at the centre of Lyotard's writing. Whether he is discussing a work of art, a literary text, theological arguments or even the end of the universe, his focus always falls upon the social and ethical issues that they evoke. Lyotard is primarily a political philosopher concerned with the ways in which our lives are organised and controlled by the societies we inhabit, and his analyses of art, literature and culture all contribute to this understanding. His relentless challenges to established beliefs, political doctrines and cultural practices make his writing continually disturbing and difficult, but at the same time exciting and inspiring.

Although he does not always use the term, much of Lyotard's work focuses on the issues arising from what is now called the postmodern. But what does this term mean? Postmodernism has acquired a rather bad name in recent years. It is often associated with a loss of values and beliefs in present-day society, and the rejection of grounds for making judgements or decisions. The postmodern writer is frequently castigated for her or his belief that in contemporary thought 'anything goes' – that the arguments one produces are no more true or just than any other sets of arguments, and that the point of thought is simply to experiment and enjoy oneself. This version of postmodernism is anathema to Lyotard's philosophy. Equally, the idea that in postmodernity truth and justice have been usurped by the self-interested propaganda of political and economic superpowers and multi-national corporations is something that Lyotard recognises but struggles against at every moment of his writing. Although he agrees that universal criteria of truth and falsity, right and wrong, and good and evil, are highly questionable and can't be taken for granted, his work constantly pursues the question of what it means to think and act responsibly in the absence of such absolute rules or universal laws. He does not just retreat into despair ('the world is incomprehensible – there is nothing I can do') or celebrate the loss of intellectual or political consensus ('there are no rules – it doesn't matter what I do'). Rather, he tenaciously searches for new ways of analysing art, culture and society in order to discover different possibilities for thought and action that just might make the world a little more just and fair. For Lyotard, then, the key task of a postmodern thinker is to confront both the apparent loss of values in 'anything goes' consumerism and the seemingly irresistible power of the market driven economies of the West that place profit before other values. These are all complex ideas, but each will be introduced clearly and in much more detail in the chapters that follow.

Because of the challenges set out in his work, Lyotard has had an impact across the Humanities. For the student of Politics or Sociology, his thought provides a series of ways in which one can begin to question established processes of organising or systematising our ideas about society. Key concepts such as the 'differend' and the 'inhuman' (which are introduced in Chapters 3 and 5 respectively) generate powerful ways to rethink social and political justice, and his insistence on the destructive effects of global capitalism make his thought absolutely relevant to today's world. The Philosopher or Critical Theorist can find in his writings thought-provoking analyses and reinterpretations of the work of some of the most important thinkers of the past and present: in particular, Immanuel Kant (1724–1804), G. W. F. Hegel (1770–1831), Friedrich Nietzsche (1844–1900), Sigmund Freud (1856–1939) and Martin Heidegger (1889–1976), as well as more recent writers such as the French psychoanalyst Jacques Lacan (1901–81) whose seminars Lyotard attended in Paris, the philosopher Gilles Deleuze (1925–95) with whom he co-wrote a number of articles, and well-known post-modernist thinkers Jean Baudrillard (1929–) and Fredric Jameson (1934–). Lyotard's wide-ranging interest in modern art and culture, as well as his theorisation of their political and philosophical import-ance, is of particular relevance to those working in Art History and Cultural Studies. And, although he does not often discuss specific literary works, Lyotard's analyses of narrative structure, aesthetics and the politics of language make him an important thinker for anybody with an interest in contemporary Literary Studies. To all of these disciplines, Lyotard brings a unique intellectual voice, a range of powerful critical tools and a demand for openness and the will to question disciplinary rules and structures.

LYOTARD'S CAREER

In a book entitled *Peregrinations: Law, Form, Event* (1988), Lyotard outlines his development towards becoming a philosopher in humorous terms. He reveals that as a child he really wanted to become either a monk, a painter or a historian. However, after attending the famous Sorbonne University in Paris, he says, that he

> soon became a husband and a father when I was still really only old enough to be a son, [and] was compelled by this drastic situation to earn a living for a family. As you can see, it was already too late to pronounce monastic vows. As for my artistic career, it was a hopeless wish because of an unfortunate lack of talent, while the obvious weakness of my memory was definitely discouraging my turn toward history. Thus I became a professor of philosophy at a lycée in Constantine, the capital of the French department of East Algeria.
>
> (Lyotard 1988b: 1–2)

On arriving in the North African country of Algeria, which was then a colony of France, Lyotard became involved in the struggles of the Algerian workers against the French rulers of the country. His experiences in this fractured country shaped much of his later work. In 1954 he became a member of a revolutionary group called *Socialisme ou Barbarie* (Socialism or Barbarism), who were attempting to reinterpret and put into practice the ideas of Karl Marx (1818–83). To summarise Marx's arguments very briefly, his political philosophy argues that in modern capitalism workers are oppressed because of their lack of control over their working conditions, and the task of the revolutionary is to help these workers rise up against their bosses and overthrow the system so that they could take control of the society they help to sustain. During his time as a revolutionary, Lyotard wrote a number of polemical essays about the situation in Algeria (which are collected in his *Political Writings* (1993c)) and became involved in the day-to-day struggles against the Algerian government, which gradually expanded into a fully-blown civil war.

However, by 1966 Lyotard had become disenchanted with Marxism and left *Socialisme ou Barbarie* to begin to develop his own political philosophy. Returning to Paris, he began to publish a number of books aimed at reworking Marxist philosophy in ways that would be more radical for contemporary politics. He played an active role in the student-led anti-government riots in May 1968, and as a result of this began to question the relations between power and knowledge in both the economy as a whole and university institutions in particular. This lead to the publication in 1974 of what is perhaps his most complex and radical book, *Libidinal Economy* (1993a), which he later referred to as 'my evil book' (1988b: 13). This book is both exhilarating and often highly disturbing, beginning with a detailed description of the way the human body can be opened up and stretched out to form a 'great ephemeral skin', going on to analyse sexual desire, and culminating in a critique of capitalism and Marxism as forms of perversion. I discuss part of this text in Chapter 5 and cite an extended passage to give a taste of the violent style in which the book is written, but what is worth pointing to here is that in many ways *Libidinal Economy*, through its rejection of systems of thought such as Marxism, paves the way for Lyotard's later work on the postmodern.

This work began in the late 1970s, and came to fruition with the publication of three key texts – *The Postmodern Condition* (1979), *Just Gaming* (1979) and *The Differend* (1983) – as well as a series of important essays on art, culture, politics and history. These are the founding texts of Lyotard's postmodern thought, and will form the main focus of this book. With their publication and subsequent translation into a range of languages, Lyotard became a major international figure whose work began to have an impact on thinkers and writers across the world.

Lyotard's later writings expand upon this work, and develop new ways of thinking about contemporary politics, art and culture. Among the most influential of these texts have been *The Inhuman: Reflections on Time* (1988), *The Postmodern Explained* (1988) that collects many of his most important and penetrating essays written in the aftermath of *The Postmodern Condition*, and *Postmodern Fables* (1993). These texts will be referred to throughout this book in order to elucidate the key ideas and approaches presented in his writing on the postmodern. They often build on ideas expounded in earlier works, but in doing so they frequently transform them to engage differently with the problems and issues he identifies as facing society.

Lyotard's last books tend to be focused more specifically on particular texts and writers. He often reworks ideas presented in his earlier texts to generate sometimes surprising rereadings of key modern writers such as the twentieth-century French novelist and adventurer André Malraux (1901–76) in *Signed, Malraux* (1996) and *Soundproof Room: Malraux's Anti-Aesthetic* (1998), and the medieval Christian theologian Saint Augustine (354–430) in the text that remained unfinished when he died, *The Confession of Augustine* (1998). These complex works are examples of postmodern criticism in action, and serve as excellent demonstrations of what is at stake in his broader theoretical formulations. They will be introduced in more detail in Chapter 6.

Lyotard's work has been shaped by a restless dissatisfaction with established ideas and a sense of the importance of justice. He continually questions accepted systems of thought and politics, and is willing to challenge even his own theories. For Lyotard, thought and action must constantly renew themselves, reflecting on their value and function, and if they are found wanting must be transformed. There is thus no 'Lyotardian system' that can be applied like a tool kit to all artistic or cultural phenomena irrespective of their differences. Rather, for Lyotard, criticism must remain responsive to what is unique in any work, and continually strive to reinvent itself in the light of new events. Like the experimental artists to whom he devotes a great deal of his time, the aim of thought for Lyotard is to open new possibilities that have the potential to change the world for the better. And it is this openness that makes his work so fascinating, challenging and inspiring.

THE MODERN AND THE POSTMODERN

Two terms that will play a central role in the discussion of Lyotard's work in this book are 'modern' and 'postmodern'. From *The Postmodern Condition* onwards, the relation between the modern and the postmodern, and the resources they offer for art, philosophy and politics have been vital for Lyotard. Neither of these terms is easy to define, and both have been debated and disagreed about at great length by critics. The aim of this book is to make Lyotard's analysis of them as clear and accessible as possible. Before looking in more specific detail at Lyotard's use of them, however, it is worth outlining briefly some of the ways in which they are currently employed by other thinkers and critics. As well as providing a working definition of the terms, this will also introduce the context of current debates about the modern and the postmodern.

MODERNISM AND POSTMODERNISM

The 'post' in 'postmodern' implies that it is a modification of the modern; in other words, that it is something that comes after it, replaces it, or disrupts it (although, as we shall see in Chapter 2, this is a formulation that Lyotard comes to question). It is therefore important to work through the relations between modernism and postmodernism, as well as modernity and postmodernity (and for many critics, these two pairs designate very different things). So, first, what do critics mean when they employ the terms 'modernism' and 'postmodernism'?

'Modernism' is generally associated with the artistic movements that took shape at the beginning of the twentieth century. In literature, novelists such as Virginia Woolf (1882–1941), James Joyce (1882–1941) and D. H. Lawrence (1885–1930) began to experiment with literary form so as to discover how new ways of narrating might allow different modes of experience to be presented. Poets such as Ezra Pound (1885–1972) and T. S. Eliot (1888–1965) tried to develop new poetic forms in which to figure the modern world. In fine art, a string of different movements from Cubism to Primitivism and Impressionism to Surrealism challenged established rules about what a work of art could or should be. Despite the differences between individual artists and movements, then, the drive of modernist art and literature has frequently been summed up by Pound's maxim 'make it new'.

Postmodern art is usually associated with more recent writers and artists, generally those working in the aftermath of the Second World War. There are a number of critics who present postmodernism as a break with the modernist cultural project. They describe postmodern art as anti-elitist and keen to break down the distinctions between high art and popular culture in a way that the modernists were not, playfully subversive of the seriousness of modernist art, and even more formally experimental in terms of their ironic use of a range of materials and styles to communicate. The Canadian critic Linda Hutcheon, for example, argues that postmodernism marks a return to concerns about the past rather than a continual drive towards newness (see Hutcheon 1988 and 1989). In postmodern art and literature, however, she argues that the recovery of the past is ironically used to disturb traditions and problematise the present. In this way writers such as Salman Rushdie describe historical events or cultural folklore in ways that make them appear strange and even humorous, and allow new questions to be asked. To cite just one example, in *Midnight's Children* (1981) Rushdie depicts India's independence from colonial Britain and its split with Pakistan, but this is done through the story of a group of children born at the moment of independence who have magical powers to shape the destiny of the nation. The novel self-consciously employs a range of traditional styles jumbled together to form its narrative, and is as concerned with the contents of pickle jars as it is with international politics and conflict.

Viewed in this way, postmodernism is thus a radicalisation of modernism in which artistic experimentation is pushed even further. For some critics (for instance Eagleton (1996) or Jameson (1991)), this experimentation goes too far and ceases to have much to do with the world or politics, becoming an escapist form of self-subversion. And yet for others (such as Hutcheon (1988 and 1989) or Elam (1992)), its disruptions of established ideas about class, gender, race and politics generally allow it to retain an important critical role.

MODERNITY AND POSTMODERNITY

The term 'modernity' is generally used to refer to something quite different from 'modernism'. If modernism is an artistic or cultural phenomenon, modernity is more concerned with the structures of social organisation (politics, the law, etc.) and knowledge (science, philosophy, etc.). It is thus a far wider category that seeks to account for all forms of social experience. Also, the time period associated with modernity tends to be much longer than the modernism of the first half of the twentieth century. Critics have disagreed quite strenuously about where to locate the origins of modernity. For some, the modern begins with the transformation of European culture during the renaissance, which saw the rise of capitalism, the spread of Protestantism and the beginnings of a destruction of feudal hierarchies. For others, the period spanning the end of the eighteenth and the beginning of the nineteenth centuries is where modernity proper comes into existence with American independence and the French Revolution that forged modern notions of the state, the industrial revolution in Britain, the transformations that took place in philosophy, and the birth of many of the modern sciences such as psychology and sociology. These are probably the two most widely

accepted versions, but some other thinkers have located the beginnings of modernity as early as the death of Christ or as late as the First
World War with its mechanisation of combat.

What all of these ideas of modernity have in common is that
they see it as a point at which human beings begin to conceive themselves differently and, in particular, begin to see themselves and their
communities in relation to change, development and history.
According to the German philosopher Jürgen Habermas, 'modernity
expresses the conviction that the future has already begun: It is the
epoch that lives for the future, that opens itself up to the novelty
of the future' (Habermas 1987: 5). In other words, modernity is
concerned with progress, whether that is the development of ideas
and technology, the generation of wealth or the movement towards
justice for all. It thinks of society as in a state of constant flux, innovation and development as changes in knowledge and technology
alter the identities and experiences of individuals and communities.
Modern systems of thought strive to find universal answers to the
questions facing society, and the different answers found by different
groups become the bases of political systems and organisations that
strive for supremacy. These systems of thought are analysed at length
by Lyotard, and his ideas about modernity are explained in detail in
Chapters 1 and 3.

Postmodernity is a challenge to this modern form of social organisation. In contemporary society, postmodern thinkers often argue,
the modern ways of organising knowledge and the world have
become outmoded and need to be rethought. For example, the
American critic Fredric Jameson argues that recent developments in
capitalism such as its international spread and its movement away
from industrial organisation in factories towards the virtual trade of
the internet and global telecommunications means that the ways
of analysing it developed in the nineteenth century by writers such as
Marx have to be rethought (see Jameson 1991). Equally, for the
French postmodernist Jean Baudrillard, these same global communication networks make all modern forms of critique outmoded, and

mean that questions about truth and justice can no longer be posed in the same ways, if they can be posed at all (see Baudrillard 1994 and 1995 for particular instances of this).

Lyotard's thinking of modernity, modernism and the postmodern draws on a number of the ideas that have just been described, and yet his analyses from *The Postmodern Condition* to *The Inhuman* challenge all of the thinkers so far mentioned. In the 'Key Ideas' section of this book, the precise nature of Lyotard's investigations of postmodernism and postmodernity will be introduced.

THIS BOOK

This book does not take a chronological approach to Lyotard's work. Instead, because most students' first encounter with Lyotard is likely to be *The Postmodern Condition*, it opens with a detailed reading of that key text with the aim of clearly setting out what is at stake in its discussion of postmodernity. The subsequent chapters will open up many of the issues raised in this analysis in order to explore in more detail Lyotard's arguments about how one might respond to this postmodern condition in philosophically, ethically and politically rigorous ways. Chapter 2 analyses a crucial category in Lyotard's work, the sublime, through a close reading of his important essay about contemporary art and culture, 'An Answer to the Question: What is the Postmodern?', and shows how Lyotard relates social notions of postmodernity to cultural postmodernism. Because Lyotard is such a politically and ethically engaged thinker, Chapter 3 examines some of his key discussions of these areas by introducing *Just Gaming* and *The Differend*. The fourth chapter asks what happens to history in the postmodern, and examines some of Lyotard's responses. Chapter 5 returns to art, and explores Lyotard's readings of a number of artists and writers, as well as describing some of the conclusions he draws about the politics of art. The final chapter of the Key Ideas section investigates Lyotard's ideas about criticism and asks what he thinks is the task of the postmodern critic. Although the book gradually builds a picture of Lyotard's work, readers might like to jump to a particular chapter if a theme is of special interest to them. Following the Key Ideas section is a short chapter that provides some details of the ways in which other critics have taken up Lyotard's ideas, and assesses the impact of his work. The book ends with some suggestions for further reading and a detailed annotated bibliography of English translations of Lyotard's major works.

It is impossible to cover all of Lyotard's work in enough detail in a short book. For this reason, I have concentrated on giving the readers the practical tools to approach Lyotard's work for themselves. This book is no substitute for reading Lyotard's own texts, however. Its aim is rather to allow readers to approach those texts with more confidence and insight. This will be a highly worthwhile exercise. Reading Lyotard is never less than exhilarating, and it is difficult to overrate the importance of his thought for understanding the culture, society and politics of the world in which we all live.

KEY IDEAS

1

THE POSTMODERN CONDITION

English-speaking readers most often associate Jean-François Lyotard's name with the term 'postmodern'. This chapter explores his contribution to the debates about postmodernism that began in the 1980s by examining his most influential intervention, *The Postmodern Condition: A Report on Knowledge*. It sets out the key arguments of that book in order to provide a way into the text for first-time readers, and then explores the implications of Lyotard's analysis for the ways we might think about and act in the contemporary world.

Towards the end of the 1970s, Lyotard was commissioned to write a report by the Council of Universities of the Provincial Government of Quebec, the French-speaking province of Canada. The subject of this report was the state of knowledge in the world's most highly developed societies at the end of the twentieth century. In other words, what Lyotard was asked to report on was the ways in which different ways of knowing about and dealing with the world – science, technology, law, the university system, etc. – are understood and valued in contemporary society.

The book that emerged at the end of this project in 1979 is *The Postmodern Condition*. It very quickly became Lyotard's most widely read, culturally significant and influential text, and also one of his most controversial works. Since publication, it has drawn commentaries from writers in a range of disciplines including Philosophy, Art History, Sociology, Politics and Literary Studies, and has set the tone for many recent accounts of postmodernity and postmodernism. In each of these areas, it has generated debates and discussions that have impacted upon the ways in which those disciplines have conducted their work. However, although many writers refer to *The Postmodern Condition* for its definition of postmodernity, the book's descriptions of contemporary culture and politics have also come in for a great deal of criticism – not least from Lyotard himself in his later writings. It is a book whose arguments we should not ignore, but whose conclusions we might wish actively to question. In order to do so, however, we need to get to grips with the detail of Lyotard's report.

The most frequently quoted and discussed assertion of the book is its definition of the postmodern as an 'incredulity toward metanarratives' (Lyotard, 1984: xxiv). This description has frequently been treated as a sound bite and all too often has been misunderstood. Rather than simply offering a brief definition of what Lyotard might be getting at when he uses terms like 'postmodern' or 'metanarrative', it is important to work out how this statement emerges from the book as a whole. The aim of this chapter, then, is to provide a basis for an understanding of what Lyotard means by describing the postmodern as 'incredulity toward metanarratives'.

A REPORT ON KNOWLEDGE

Probably the best place to begin trying to discover what *The Postmodern Condition* is about is by looking closely at its subtitle: *A Report on Knowledge*. As with all of Lyotard's work, it is just as important to pay attention to the *way* in which he writes, as it is to understand what is written *about*, and the subtitle of the book immediately gives crucial clues about both its form and content.

First, it is described as a 'report'. Generally, a report is a formal statement of the results of an investigation into a specific subject, usually undertaken by experts, that draws together the range of available evidence in order to set out specific conclusions. *The Postmodern Condition*'s status as a report is evident in the way it is written. One of the first things that is noticeable on reading the text is the amount of evidence that is presented in the footnotes, of which there are over 200 referring to an even larger number of other books, essays, lectures and government documents from many European and American countries. Lyotard synthesises this vast range of material in a text that is often abstract and contains only relatively few concrete examples of specific events. In other words, the main text of *The Postmodern Condition* provides a summary account of the documents mentioned in its notes. Its aim is to discover underlying trends and relationships between the different sources, and to trace out as clearly as possible the development of knowledge in contemporary Western societies.

The other key term in the subtitle is 'knowledge'. Lyotard states that he is studying the 'condition of knowledge in the most highly developed societies' (1984: xxiii), but what does this mean? The idea of a report on, for example, the state of the public transport system in London or a child's progress during their first year at school is quite straightforward. In both cases there is obvious evidence that can be called upon to support the conclusions: the lateness of the average bus, perhaps, or the marks awarded in end of year maths tests. But what does it mean to report on the 'condition of knowledge'? Clearly, this isn't a question of how much we know nowadays: *The Postmodern Condition* is not just a list of the recent developments in physics, zoology or computer science. What is at stake is much more fundamental, and much more important.

According to Lyotard, the focus is the 'nature' and 'status' of knowledge: what knowledge is, and how it is generated, organised and employed in contemporary societies. In other words, *The Postmodern Condition* is a report about the ways in which advanced societies treat education, science, technology, research and development. Lyotard investigates which sorts of knowledge count as valuable, how that knowledge is communicated, who has access to it and what it is used for, who determines and controls the flow of knowledge, and how it shapes our lives and experiences of the world.

The central question of *The Postmodern Condition*'s 'report on knowledge' is thus, how are the lives and identities of people constructed by contemporary structures of knowing? According to Lyotard, this is a fundamental question because 'the status of knowledge is altered as our societies enter what is known as the postindustrial age and cultures enter what is known as the postmodern age' (1984: 3). This is the main hypothesis of the book, and the aim of the text is to test whether it is correct and to describe its implications.

POSTMODERN KNOWLEDGE

Lyotard argues that the advances in communications that have taken place since the Second World War have affected not just how knowledge is transmitted but also the status of knowledge itself. It is not just that we can store more information on computers, and send messages across the world quickly by post, telephone and now email. It is also that these changes in storage and communication are transforming how we use and value knowledge: 'the miniaturization and commercialization of machines is already changing the way in which learning is acquired, classified, made available and exploited' (1984: 4). In other words, in what Lyotard calls the 'postmodern condition', knowledge itself has changed.

Lyotard demonstrates that knowledge has become a commodity that is bought and sold on the market, and is also the basis of power in society: 'Knowledge in the form of an informational commodity indispensable to productive power is already, and will continue to be, a major – perhaps *the* major – stake in the worldwide competition for power' (1984: 5). The most powerful nations are the ones who have the greatest knowledge resources: those with the best technology, the most advanced communications and weapons systems, the most highly developed medicines and the means to collect the most detailed information about their competitors. The global competition for power is now fought out as a battle for knowledge just as it used to be for resources like coal, gas and oil. Lyotard foresees a time when nations may literally go to war over knowledge, just as they have fought over land and raw materials such as oil in the past (1984: 5).

On the other hand, Lyotard argues that states are beginning to lose their positions of power in the world as the most important bodies in this new knowledge-based economy. Multi-national corporations such as computer firms, oil companies and the pharmaceutical industry are replacing them as the key players as knowledge itself becomes a commodity. These multi-nationals fund vast amounts of research and use the patent laws to claim ownership of the knowledge generated by it, which can then be put to use to make money. Lyotard's argument here seems particularly prophetic of the changes that many commentators have identified as taking place during the 1980s and 1990s: international corporations' influence has penetrated to the very heart of the decision making processes of national governments, and international treaties (often drawn up by boards staffed with representatives from those corporations) now threaten to dictate the legal systems and cultural policies of countries throughout the world (for accessible and influential accounts of this process see, for example, Naomi Klein's *No Logo* (2000) or George Monbiot's *Captive State* (2000)).

To give just one example of this process, in 2001 the South African government was taken to court by a group of pharmaceutical companies because they claimed that it wasn't respecting the patents they had taken out on anti-AIDS medicines. The cost of producing the actual medicines was minimal so they could be manufactured cheaply in South Africa, but what the companies were protecting was the investments they had made in researching and developing these medicines. In this case then, it was knowledge itself that was the commodity for the multinationals. The South African government, which claimed it was trying to save the lives of its citizens without bankrupting the country, were accused of stealing knowledge and cheating these companies out of their profits. A compromise was eventually reached, which meant that the medicines could be bought in Africa for slightly less money, but the fact that a state could be taken to court by private companies for breach of patent shows how politically charged the ownership of knowledge has become.

Another thing this example demonstrates is that science and knowledge are not separate from politics and ethics, but are political through and through. The changes in the status of knowledge that are now taking place therefore mark a transformation in the nature of society and human experience. It is precisely this political transformation that is at stake in Lyotard's report on knowledge in *The Postmodern Condition*. The method he chooses to analyse the changes in knowledge and political organisation that form the condition of postmodernity draws on the idea of 'language games'.

LANGUAGE GAMES, LEGITIMATION AND IDENTITY

Lyotard argues that there are two key aspects to the development of knowledge that was described in the last section. The first is that advances in science have wider implications in society. This should be clear from the example of AIDS in South Africa. The research of the drugs companies is immediately tied to questions of money, power and human suffering; it is not just a question of scientific discovery for its own sake. In general terms, this indicates that an advance in research might well have implications for other areas of social policy, as well as for people's everyday life. The second aspect of the development of knowledge follows from this: there are different types of knowledge at work in society, they have different criteria for being categorised as useful or true, and they must be examined in different ways.

In *The Postmodern Condition*, Lyotard differentiates between two major types of discourse: scientific knowledge and narrative knowledge. He argues that 'scientific knowledge does not represent the totality of knowledge; it has always existed in addition to [. . .] narrative' (1984: 7). For Lyotard, narratives are the stories that communities tell themselves to explain their present existence, their history and ambitions for the future. Although the term 'narrative' is commonly associated with literary fiction, all forms of discourse employ narratives to present their ideas. Examples of this might include History that constructs narratives of the past, Psychology that tells stories about the self, or Sociology that depicts different social formations and their effects on individuals. In the same way, scientific statements are presented through types of narrative that describe the physical world. In order to explain and justify their discoveries, even mathematical sciences are forced to turn their equations into narratives that explain the implications of their findings. In this way, narrative stands at the basis of human experience and society: it tells us who we are, and allows us to express what we believe and aspire to.

Of course, the different types of narrative used in different discourses follow different rules. The different discourses that make up a society's knowledge – be they physics, chemistry, literature, laws, customs, or even gossip – all have different sets of rules for what count as legitimate statements. In *The Postmodern Condition*, Lyotard refers to these different discourses as 'language games', a term he draws from the highly influential Austrian philosopher Ludwig Wittgenstein.

Drawing this notion of language games from Wittgenstein's philosophy, Lyotard makes three observations about them. First, that the rules of a language game are 'the object of a contract, explicit or not, between the players' (1984: 10). This means that the rules of a particular language game like poetry or biology are not natural but determined by a community. Second, that 'every utterance should

WITTGENSTEIN AND LANGUAGE GAMES

Ludwig Wittgenstein (1889–1951) was born in Vienna, and moved to Cambridge in 1911 where he began to develop groundbreaking analyses of logic and language. His most influential books are *Tractatus Logico-Philosophicus* (1921), in which he argues that many seemingly intractable philosophical problems arise from misleading pictures of the workings of language, and the posthumously published *Philosophical Investigations* (1953). In the later book, Wittgenstein asserts that meaning is pragmatic (based on the use of words in specific situations, and coming from the Greek word '*pragma*' meaning 'deed') rather than natural or fixed. He argues that, 'the meaning of a word is its use in language' (1967: 20), which implies that words gain their meaning from what they do rather than being fixed labels for things. Language is therefore an active part of our day-to-day existence, and we use words in order to have effects on the people and things around us. In order to explain this idea, Wittgenstein developed the theory of 'language games'.

Like normal games, there are a variety of language games that may not always have rules in common. For example, in chess there are rules that allow us to move the pieces in certain ways, set out our objectives for victory and make certain moves illegal. In the same way, in science certain types of statement can be made about the world and certain aims and rules are involved in scientific enquiry and experimentation. The success or failure of a given statement is thus determined by how well it works within the rules of the language game in which it occurs. In each of the different language games, the rules are a pragmatic agreement between the players (for example, between the members of the scientific community about what counts as proper research), and the aim is usually to further the aims of the community that the game sets up.

be thought of as a "move" in a game' (1984: 10). And third, that 'if there are no rules there is no game, that even an infinitesimal modification of one rule alters the nature of the game' (1984: 10). In other words, that all language 'moves' obey rules, but the games of which they are a part are open to change and influence by other games or even as the result of the moves themselves.

Lyotard argues that the outcome of these three observations is that the 'social bond is composed of language "moves"' (1984: 11). The very structure of society is made up of the statements made in it and the rules it develops to decide whether particular moves are legitimate or illegitimate. Just as different types of games have distinct sets of rules, different societies have diverse forms of politics, law and legitimation. As subjects, we exist within this series of language games, whose different sets of rules make up who we are. According to Lyotard,

> A *self* does not amount to much, but no self is an island . . . [E]ven before he is born, if only by virtue of the name he is given, the human child is already positioned as the referent of a story recounted by those around him, in relation to which he will inevitably chart his course.
>
> (1984: 15)

The organisation of knowledge in society thereby determines the identity – the self-image, the ideas and aspirations – of the people that make it up. A question immediately arises, however: how do we understand this 'organisation of knowledge'? How are the different language games related to each other in a society? How is their importance to that society decided? And why do different societies have different ways of organising the language games that make them up? For Lyotard, the answer to this question lies in the term mentioned at the beginning of this chapter. The organisation of the narratives and language games is performed by meta-narratives.

METANARRATIVES

As the terms implies (the prefix, 'meta', denotes something of a higher order – so, for example, in linguistics a metalanguage is a language used to describe the workings of another language), a meta-narrative sets out the rules of narratives and language games. This means that the metanarrative organises language games, and determines the success or failure of each statement or language 'move' that takes place in them. In *The Postmodern Condition*, Lyotard presents a number of metanarratives, and describes the different ways in which they organise knowledge. The basis of modernity is, for Lyotard, a certain type of metanarrative organisation. In order to understand why he defines the postmodern as 'incredulity toward metanarratives' (1984: xxiv), then, it is useful to come to terms with what these metanarratives are and how they work.

Lyotard argues that from the earliest human societies right up until the present, narrative has continued to be the 'quintessential form of customary knowledge' (1984: 19). As an example of the most tradi-tional form of narrative organisation, Lyotard introduces the Cashina-hua, a tribe from the upper reaches of the Amazon in South America. The stories of this tribe follow a fixed formula for narrating the adven-tures of their people. They begin with the phrase, 'Here is the story of –, as I have always heard it told. I will tell it to you in my turn. Listen.' In this way, the story is always one handed down from the past, and is passed on in the present to the community. At the end of the story comes another formulaic statement: 'Here ends the story of – . The man who has told it to you is – (Cashinahua name), or to the whites – (Spanish or Portuguese name)' (see 1984: 20–1). With this statement, the storyteller links himself with the ancestral hero: the two names appear together as a bond between past and present.

This form of storytelling organises the rituals and structure of the Cashinahua society. They share their historical knowledge through the tales, construct their identity as a group, and order their society through the rules about who is allowed to tell and listen to the stories. According to Lyotard, 'The knowledge transmitted by these narrations . . . determines in a single stroke what one must say in order to be heard, what one must listen to in order to speak, and what role one must play . . . to be the object of a narrative' (1984: 21). Each member of the community is given a place in the system as speaker, audience or hero of the tales, and their identity and desires are shaped by it.

According to Lyotard, this is the sort of metanarrative organisation that is common in pre-modern cultures. In contrast to this form, which is based on the relationship between past (the stories themselves) and present (their narration), Lyotard describes another form of metanarrative: the grand narratives of modernity. For Lyotard, modernity is defined by its reliance upon grand narratives that depict human progress. Their difference from traditional metanarratives is that they point towards a future in which the problems facing a society (which is most often thought of as all of humanity) will be resolved. He identifies two key types of modern metanarrative in *The Postmodern Condition*: the speculative grand narrative and the grand narrative of emancipation (or freedom).

The speculative grand narrative originates in the German philosophy of the early nineteenth century, which found its most detailed form in the writings of G. W. F. Hegel.

HEGEL

Georg Wilhelm Friedrich Hegel (1770–1831) is one of the most influential thinkers in the history of philosophy. In his writing, modernity finds its clearest and most powerful formulation. For Hegel, the world is capable of being comprehended by philosophical thought. This thought, called by Hegel the 'speculative dialectic', presents reality and history as rationally explicable through a system of ideas. Hegel's dialectic describes a process of constantly overturning the relations between ideas and material reality. The dialectic involves three steps: (1) a concept is taken as fixed and clear, but (2) on closer analysis contradictions emerge in it which, when worked through, result (3) in a higher concept that includes both the original and its contradictions. This means that knowledge is constantly progressing. The goal of knowledge is what Hegel calls the 'Absolute'. With the Absolute, all contradictions and oppositions between ideas and reality are reconciled in a system of philosophical knowledge. This idea of the philosophical system is set out in a number of Hegel's texts, including *Phenomenology of Spirit* (1807), *Science of Logic* (1812–16) and the *Encyclopaedia of the Philosophical Sciences* (1817–27).

The central idea of the speculative grand narrative is that human life, or 'Spirit' as Hegel calls it, progresses by increasing its knowledge. All the different language games are brought together by philosophy in order to present a 'universal "history" of spirit' (1984: 34). All knowledge is thus related in a system of philosophy and, according to Lyotard, 'True knowledge . . . is composed of reported statements [that] are incorporated into the metanarrative of a subject that guarantees their legitimacy' (1984: 35). For the speculative grand narrative, all possible statements are brought together under a single metanarrative, and their truth and value are judged according to its rules. This account of the speculative narrative emerges from Hegel's argument that 'the True is the whole' (Hegel, 1977: 11), which means that the truth or falsity of any statement or language game is determined by its relation to the whole of knowledge. And this whole of knowledge is the speculative grand narrative.

The second type of modern metanarrative is the grand narrative of emancipation. Unlike the speculative grand narrative in which knowledge is an end in itself, this grand narrative presents knowledge as being valuable because it is the basis of human freedom. Here, 'humanity is the hero of liberty. All peoples have a right to science' (1984: 31). This grand narrative begins for Lyotard with the French Revolution in 1789. In post-revolutionary France, the idea of universal education was seen as a means of freeing all citizens from the shackles of mysticism and domination. In this narrative, knowledge is the basis of freedom from oppression, and the developments in knowledge are valued because they set humanity free from suffering. Here, then, the basis of truth is morality: 'Knowledge is no longer the subject, but in the service of the subject' (1984: 36). The grand narrative of emancipation has taken many different forms over the past few hundred years. Its Enlightenment version focuses on the idea of the freedom of people from religious superstitions that curtail their lives and place power in the hands of the priests. The Marxist version, on the other hand, focuses on the freedom of the workers from exploitation by their masters and the development of their ability to control their own lives. The aim of this type of grand narrative, in whatever form it occurs, is thus the emancipation of an enlightened humanity from dogma, mysticism, exploitation and suffering.

These are the two key grand narratives discussed in *The Postmodern Condition*. While there are significant differences between them, they share a similar structure. In each, all the different areas of knowledge are brought together to achieve a goal that is projected forward into the future as being the answer to the problems facing society. Under a grand narrative, all the social institutions such as law, education and technology combine to strive for a common goal for all humanity: absolute knowledge or universal emancipation. Knowledge thus acquires a vocation and a role for the greater good.

According to Lyotard, though, the transformations in knowledge that have taken place during the last half-century have thrown these grand narratives into doubt. Nowadays, knowledge is organised differently:

> In contemporary society and culture – postindustrial society, post-modern culture – the question of the legitimation of knowledge is formulated in different terms. The grand narrative has lost its credibility, regardless of whether it is a speculative narrative or a narrative of emancipation.
>
> (1984: 37)

Nowadays, Lyotard argues, knowledge is no longer organised towards the fulfilment of universal human goals. Instead, postmodern knowledge is valued in terms of its efficiency and profitability in a market-driven global economy. It is this transformation of knowledge, marked by the 'incredulity toward metanarratives', that defines Lyotard's notion of the postmodern. So what, then, is the postmodern condition? We are now in a position to begin to answer that question.

THE POSTMODERN CONDITION

For Lyotard, the global spread of capitalism and the rapid developments in science and technology since the Second World War have put an end to grand narratives. As he says in a later essay called 'Apostil on Narratives', 'the project of modernity . . . has not been forsaken or forgotten, but destroyed, "liquidated"' (1992: 18). I will discuss this sense of the 'liquidation' of grand narratives in more detail in Chapter 4, which focuses on Lyotard's analyses of historical change in more detail. What is clear in *The Postmodern Condition*, however, is that capitalism has become the driving force of knowledge, research and development in contemporary society: 'In matters of social justice and scientific truth alike, the legitimation of . . . power is based on its optimising the system's performance – efficiency' (1984: xxiv). This drive for efficiency lies at the heart of capitalism: the aim of research and development is to make production and consumption cheaper and quicker so as to maximise the potential for profit.

For Lyotard, the unrelenting spread of capitalism has destroyed the traditional social bonds that link all of humanity in the grand narratives of progress. Truth, the basis of the speculative grand narrative, and justice, the goal of the grand narrative of emancipation, no longer have the universal appeal they did for modernity. This fundamentally changes the nature and status of knowledge in contemporary society.

This change affects not just research and development, but identity itself. Located in a multiplicity of language games that no longer follow a single metanarrative, an individual's identity becomes dispersed:

> The social subject itself seems to dissolve in the dissemination of language games. The social bond is linguistic, but is not woven with a single thread. It is a fabric formed by the intersection of at least two (and in reality an indeterminate number) of language games, obeying different rules.

> (1984: 40)

With the destruction of the grand narratives, there is no longer any unifying identity for the subject or society. Instead individuals are the sites where ranges of conflicting moral and political codes intersect, and the social bond is fragmented. This process is most aptly summed up in the infamous statement made in the 1980s by Margaret Thatcher, then British Prime Minister, when she claimed that there is no such thing as society, only individuals. Whether this is true or not, the fact that such a claim can be taken seriously illustrates the transformation that has taken place.

In the light of this fragmentation of society, and the simultaneous disruption of traditional forms of justice, culture and identity, there are two types of possible response. The first is the approach taken by the contemporary German theorist, Jürgen Habermas. Habermas sees modernity as an incomplete project and wants to further its aims by overcoming the disintegration of contemporary society. This must be done, he argues, by striving to reach consensus between the different language games through negotiation (see Habermas 1987).

Lyotard's aim is the opposite of this. He sees the grand narratives themselves as having always been politically problematic; for example, the universal ideas of reason and freedom from superstition provided a moral basis for colonial domination through capitalist expansion and missionary terrorism in Africa and the Middle East (see Lyotard 1993: 165–326). He thus argues that the best means to resist the globalisation of capitalism is by increasing the fragmentation of language games. As language games are linked to identity, Lyotard argues that the wider range of different language games that are considered legitimate within society, the more open and pluralist that society can become. The main threat facing postmodern society is the reduction of knowledge to a single system whose only criterion is efficiency. He sees the capitalist system as 'a vanguard machine dragging humanity after it, dehumanising it' (1984: 63) as all knowledge is judged in terms of its financial value and its technological efficiency. For Lyotard, the great threat of capitalism is its potential to reduce everything to its own system. Capitalism, he argues, 'necessarily entails a certain level of terror: be operational . . . or disappear' (1984: xxiv). The threat faced by non-efficient knowledge – non-profitable or non-technological – is that it will disappear as it ceases to be supported or respected.

Postmodernity is not, however, a condition without hope. Although Lyotard does not propose a new grand narrative to replace those of modernity, what he begins to suggest at the end of the book is how the capitalist system contains the seeds of its own disruption. He argues that although universal consensus is no longer possible, 'justice as a value is neither outmoded nor suspect. We must thus arrive at an idea and practice of justice that is not linked to that of consensus' (1984: 66). This practice focuses on the individual 'little narratives' and their differences from each other, the fact that they are not all reducible to the criterion of efficiency. Once the grand narratives have fallen away, we are left only with the diverse range of language games, and the aim of postmodern criticism should be to do justice to them by allowing them to be heard in their own terms.

As a model for this criticism, Lyotard describes the ways in which discoveries in modern science have the potential to transform the whole nature of scientific knowledge by opening up new language games. Perhaps the most obvious example of one of these transformations is the discovery in quantum physics that at a sub-atomic level the standard laws of physics cease to work and one is left only with probabilities about the movement of particles. Quantum physics thereby introduces a new language game (the language of probability) into scientific discourse that transforms the range of ways in which it can describe the world.

Lyotard argues that this sort of scientific investigation 'suggests a model of legitimation that has nothing to do with maximised performance, but has as its basis difference understood as paralogy' (1984: 60). By paralogy, which can literally be defined as bad or false logic, Lyotard is describing the way in which a language move has the potential to break the rules of an existing game (which is why it seems bad or false) in such a way that a new game needs to be developed. So, for example, with the introduction of quantum physics some of the rules of scientific enquiry have to alter so that it does not become self-contradictory. Lyotard argues that systems of knowledge, moreover, are always being disturbed, and that with paralogy

[i]t is necessary to posit the existence of a power that destabilizes the capacity for explanation, manifested in the promulgation of new norms for understanding or, if one prefers, in a proposal to establish new rules circumscribing a new field of research for the language of science.

(1984: 61)

This 'power that destabilizes the capacity for explanation' is central to all of Lyotard's thought, and takes on many different forms in his texts. In later chapters of this book the destabilising power will be linked to terms such as the sublime, the differend, the sign and the event. What it allows him to argue in each case, though, is that systems of knowledge such as the speculative grand narrative or international capitalism are always open to disruptive critique, and that it is the task of the critic to pinpoint the destabilising power in them. Unfortunately, this is not as straightforward as it may at first sound, and the aim of the following chapters is to examine some of the different ways in which Lyotard shows that this resistance and critique should take place. How, in other words, Lyotard constructs the idea of a postmodern politics.

SUMMARY

In *The Postmodern Condition: A Report on Knowledge* Lyotard examines the ways in which the nature and status of knowledge have changed in contemporary society. He argues that the sort of grand narratives that used to organise knowledge, categorise its usefulness for humanity and direct it towards a goal have lost their power in the postmodern world. All that remains as an organising principle are the criteria of efficiency and profit that are propagated by capitalism's global markets. In order to present this case, Lyotard develops a method of analysing knowledge through language games and meta-narratives, which provide sets of rules to determine which sorts of statement are legitimate and which are not in each particular field of knowledge or experience. Instead of reducing everything to questions of efficiency and profit, Lyotard argues for the importance of respecting the differences between language games, and thus for the vital role that resistance to universal systems of organisation plays today. In order to achieve this potential for resistance, he argues that it is necessary to strive for paralogy within the system rather than attempting to create a new grand narrative that will bring all language games into line in a different way.

2

ART, THE SUBLIME
AND THE POSTMODERN

The last chapter ended by arguing that *The Postmodern Condition* finds in scientific paralogy a useful model for resistance to the comodification of life and culture in contemporary global capitalism. Paralogy breaks the rules of established ways of discussing and representing the world in scientific enquiry, and opens up new horizons for thought. In science, paralogy occurs when a new mode of scientific discourse alters the rules of science's language games and allows different ways of thinking to emerge. In his later writings, Lyotard retains this notion of the importance of questioning the assumptions of authoritative language games, and yet his focus tends to be based much more on the radical political potential of art, or rather, more specifically, the philosophical category called aesthetics.

In an essay from 1982 entitled 'An Answer to the Question: What is the Postmodern?', Lyotard focuses his attention on the potential of postmodern art and literature to challenge established beliefs about representation and reality. What makes this essay crucial to understanding Lyotard's thought is that its focus on aesthetics produces an account of postmodernism that is more nuanced and complex than that presented in *The Postmodern Condition*. This chapter

AESTHETICS

Aesthetics has two senses in philosophy. The restricted sense is that it is the study of beauty in art and nature. More generally, though, it refers to the whole process of human perception and sensation: those feelings of pleasure and pain that are not simply reducible to clearly defined intellectual concepts. Aesthetics as a particular discipline of enquiry emerged during the eighteenth century with the work of the German philosopher, Alexander Baumgarten (1714–62). Since then, it has formed a key part of the work of many of the thinkers discussed in this book, particularly Immanuel Kant whose *Critique of Judgement* (1790) provides one of the most influential analyses of aesthetics in both the specifically art-based and the more general sense of the term, and G. W. F. Hegel whose *Aesthetics: Lectures on Fine Art* (1835) focuses, as its title suggests, on the aesthetics of art. In debates around modernity and postmodernity, aesthetics can be used in both the restrictive sense of a philosophy of art and in the more general sense of an account of perception and feeling.

will lay out Lyotard's argument in this important essay, elucidate the developments in his thinking about the postmodern, and introduce an aesthetic category that he employs there and returns to constantly in his later work. This category is the sublime. I will explain and discuss the sublime in more detail later in the chapter, but first it is useful to set the context for Lyotard's employment of it by examining the key arguments of the essay.

If *The Postmodern Condition* reports on the state of knowledge and science under modern capitalism, 'An Answer to the Question: What is the Postmodern?' discusses the position and value of art in contemporary culture. Lyotard argues that we have entered what he calls a 'moment of relaxation' (1992: 1) as experimental work in art and literature faces a critical backlash that disparages the challenges that have been presented to culture and tradition by avant-garde artists throughout the twentieth century.

AVANT-GARDE

This term, taken from the French, literally refers to the vanguard of an army that enters the battle first. Experimental artists appropriated it early in the twentieth century to describe their own positions in relation to the rest of society. For them, art led the way in generating and presenting new ideas and possibilities for culture and society. The French poet and critic André Breton (1896–1966), who wrote two manifestos that explained the aims of the avant-garde movement called Surrealism, captures some of the typical aims of avant-garde groups in a statement from the 'First Manifesto of Surrealism':

> Surrealism, such as I conceive of it, asserts our complete *nonconformism* ... The world is only relatively in tune with thought, and incidents of this kind are only the most obvious episodes of a war in which I am proud to be participating. Surrealism is the 'invisible ray' which will one day enable us to overcome our opponents.
>
> (Harrison and Wood 1992: 438)

It is this idea of 'non-conformism', as well as the sense of disrupting established ideas of the world, that Lyotard picks up on and investigates in his writing on the postmodern.

Throughout his career, Lyotard has been a champion of avant-garde art (see, for example, his work on Marcel Duchamp (Lyotard 1990b), Barnett Newman (Lyotard 1991a) or Jacques Monory (Lyotard 1998)), and his discussion of postmodernism in 'An Answer to the Question' is based upon a defence of the continuing importance of avant-garde experimentation.

The essay begins by listing a series of criticisms recently launched against experimentation in the arts and humanities, but comes to focus most decisively on Jürgen Habermas's analysis of art and modernity in the essay entitled 'Modernity: an Unfinished Project' (translated in Passerin d'Entrèves and Benhabib 1996: 38–55). Habermas's opposition to Lyotard was introduced briefly in the last chapter. However, it is worth expanding on here as the differences between their arguments make the position that each holds and the alternatives of modern and postmodern approaches to aesthetics easier to understand.

In 'Modernity: an Unfinished Project', Habermas shares Lyotard's belief in the fragmentation of culture under contemporary capitalism, but his analysis of its relation to art could not be more different. This disagreement between the two writers is not just an esoteric and academic dispute about the nature of avant-garde art. Nor is it simply a fashionable spat about which works in the contemporary art scene are good or bad. Rather, for both Habermas and Lyotard, art has the potential to generate political action, and to resist the dehumanising impact of our free-market oriented culture. In other words, their respective ideas of the place and role of art rest on particular assumptions about knowledge and morality, and point towards different modes of thinking about politics, identity and culture.

HABERMAS AND THE UNFINISHED PROJECT OF MODERNITY

Habermas argues that under the influence of contemporary capitalism human reason has become instrumental, by which he means that developments in knowledge are valued for their economic and political efficiency rather than their potential to improve human life. Or, in other words, that scientific and technological invention has become an end in itself, and takes little notice of the effect these inventions might have on individuals' lives. The result of this, according to Habermas, is that everyday life has split off from the various expert cultures (such as science, technology, art, and even party politics), and that the layperson can no longer understand or take part in these spheres that crucially affect her or his whole existence by laying down the rules that shape society.

Habermas argues that one should struggle against this fracturing of social life, and that the way in which this can best be achieved is by retaining the notion of emancipation (one of the grand narratives of modernity described in the last chapter) as a means of reconciling the different language games that make up a culture. It is in this sense that, for Habermas, modernity is an unfinished project: universal emancipation is possible but has not been fully achieved, and we should continue to strive for it. To this end, Habermas develops a theory of 'communicative action', a democratic notion that aims to create a public space where all peoples can enter freely and equally into discussion with the aim of reaching a consensus about the rules and laws (both moral and political) that should govern conduct in the world. For Habermas, the basis of rationality is not individual minds but rather the ability to communicate. He argues that communication rests on the possibility of reaching a consensus between participants, and that the aim of theory is to set up the conditions where genuine communication can take place.

'Modernity: an Unfinished Project' is a polemically written essay, which ends with an attack on those thinkers, Lyotard included, who for one reason or other celebrate the fragmentation of modern life. Habermas sees them as 'neo-conservatives': as thinkers who have turned their backs upon the idea of emancipation linked to the narratives of modernity. One of the key areas of 'neo-conservative' thought that he criticises is its account of aesthetics and art. According to Habermas, art must be thought of as a part of the project of emancipation, and its role of helping people to understand and act in the world around them should be recaptured from the experts and critics whose discussions of art are incomprehensible to those who don't share their level of specialist education.

For Habermas, modernism marks the quintessence of emancipatory art. He argues that the beginning of the twentieth century saw numerous attempts by the avant-garde to disrupt social consensus and offer new ways of acting by forging new links with the past to redefine contemporary culture. However, he argues that these modernist attempts have been overcome by, and failed in the face of, a new conservatism (of which postmodernism is one key aspect) which seeks to impose new disciplines and restraints on both artistic culture and society itself. With this view of the state of art in mind, Habermas describes what he sees its political potential to be:

> when [an experience of art] is related to problems of life or used in an exploratory fashion to illuminate a life-historical situation, it enters a language game which is no longer that of art criticism proper. In this case aesthetic experience not only revitalises those need interpretations in the light of which we perceive our world, but also influences our cognitive interpretations and our normative expectations, and thus alters the way in which all these moments *refer back and forth* to one another.
>
> (Passerin d'Entrèves and Benhabib 1996: 51)

What he means by this is that art, when it is rescued from the expert spheres of artistic or literary criticism, becomes a means by which people can perceive their social position, and articulate their needs and desires. In other words, what is important about art is not its aesthetic impact, but rather the ways in which particular works can be put to use by people to gain a greater understanding of their social position and the opportunities open to them.

Perhaps the most straightforward illustrations of this process of appropriation of art to shed light on social existence can be found in the dramatic device of a play within a play. In *Hamlet*, for example, Hamlet persuades the actors to perform 'The Mousetrap' in order to discover whether Claudius has killed the Prince's father: prevented from directly accusing the king, or even asking him openly about his guilt, Hamlet employs theatre to intervene in the political situation of the play. A slightly different example might be found in Timberlake Wertenbaker's play *Our Country's Good*, premiered at London's Royal Court Theatre in 1988. Here, a group of convicts transported to Australia at the end of the eighteenth century put on a production of a famous play by George Farquhar, *The Recruiting Officer* (1706). The convicts, through rehearsing and performing this play, link it with their own position as people transported for life, and generate a sense of self-identity as a community. In each of these cases it little matters whether the performance is aesthetically pleasing or artistically polished, what is important is the impact that the play within the play has on the social structure and politics of the dramatic world in which it occurs. Each of the performances sets up a space in which it becomes possible to find a way to represent social needs and aspirations, to generate a sense of community, and to strive for justice. For Habermas, this is the aim of art: to anticipate in aesthetic presentation the possibility of rational communication taking place, and to create a space in which ideas of justice and community can be explored.

'AN ANSWER TO THE QUESTION: WHAT IS THE POSTMODERN?'

In his response to 'Modernity: an Unfinished Project', Lyotard argues that what Habermas requires from the experience of art is that it 'form a bridge over the gap separating the discourses of knowledge, ethics, and politics, thus opening the way for a unity of experience' (1992: 3). In effect, Lyotard accuses Habermas of attempting to reconcile the language games of knowledge, morality and politics through art's 'communicative action' in a way that modern politics and theory has, through its continual efforts to do the same thing over the past few hundred years, shown to be impossible. The difficulty of this reconciliation is most apparent in the work of the eighteenth-century philosopher, Immanuel Kant.

KANT

Immanuel Kant (1724–1804) is a thinker who is vitally important for discussions of modernity and the postmodern, and has a crucial influence on the development of Lyotard's work. In his three *Critiques* (of 'pure reason', 'practical reason' and 'judgement'), Kant splits human experience into three different spheres – knowledge, morality and taste – which correspond to three types of philosophical enquiry: epistemology (the theory of what it is to know), ethics (the rules about how one should act) and aesthetics.

The first *Critique*, the *Critique of Pure Reason* (1781), (1787), asks how we can have knowledge of the world. Kant undertakes a transcendental enquiry into experience (which means an enquiry that seeks to discover the conditions that make it possible for experiences to occur). He argues that all knowledge must be based on experience. In other words, knowledge arises from the relation between mental concepts and physical perceptions. For this reason, Kant argues that knowledge only occurs within the 'limits of experience', and that claims about what exceeds experience are untrustworthy. He thus distinguishes between concepts, which are based on experience, and ideas, which provide the conditions for concepts but do not have corresponding objects. Ideas, he argues, regulate the way our concepts work, but cannot themselves be presented. So, for example, history (as the total movement of the past and all of its different relations) is an idea because it cannot be represented as a whole by any object or experience, whereas the first moon landing can be identified with a date, a country, particular astronauts, etc., so it can be brought under a concept or concepts, and can be thought of as a historical event because we have the idea of history to categorise it.

In the second *Critique*, the *Critique of Practical Reason* (1788), Kant is concerned to explain ethics. He sets out to deduce the fundamental principle of morality, and argues that we can call an action good only if the motive behind it is just. The basis for his notion of the just motive is the 'categorical imperative': the idea that one should act only on a maxim that one would want to be applied universally. So, for example, telling lies is wrong because if lying were universal there would be no possibility of truth and thus no point in communicating at all. According to the criteria of the first *Critique*, then, the categorical imperative is an idea rather than a concept: it regulates all aspects of behaviour but does not itself describe particular situations or actions.

Between epistemology and ethics, Kant draws a division that cannot be crossed. Because he argues that knowledge is bound by the 'limits of experience' which cannot be exceeded without falling prey to illusions and errors, he makes room for a separate ethical realm in which human freedom rests upon a 'categorical imperative' that is not reducible to knowledge because it is not generated by experience (it is a formal law, an idea, that is 'applied' to experience).

Kant's aim in the third *Critique*, the *Critique of Judgement* (1790), is to bridge the gap between epistemology and ethics opened up by the first two *Critiques*. In the first part of the book he discusses aesthetics as a possible means of achieving this. Since the publication of the third *Critique*, there has been a great deal of debate among philosophers about whether this attempt was, or ever could be, successful. This is the central stake in the discussion between Habermas and Lyotard: the former thinks art can present the possibility of reconciliation between knowledge and morality; the latter disagrees entirely and argues that art has a very different task.

Lyotard accuses Habermas of believing that art can reconcile epistemology and ethics in order to achieve the political consensus of rational communicative action. This, he claims, is not possible: Habermas's idea of consensual communication will never be more than a 'transcendental illusion'. As Lyotard argues, it is not the aim of art to effect a 'reconciliation between "language games". Kant . . . knew that they are separated by an abyss and that only a transcendental illusion (Hegel's) can hope to totalise them into a real unity. But he also knew that the price of this illusion is terror. The nineteenth and twentieth centuries have given us our fill of terror'

(1992: 15–16). Here, Lyotard links the idea of philosophical totality, the idea (or illusion) of being able to explain everything in a single grand narrative, with political totalitarianism and terror. Political movements in the twentieth century such as Nazism or Soviet Communism under Stalin present views that explain the world totally, and anything or anyone that does not fit into these systems is forcibly suppressed, excluded or wiped out. I shall discuss this idea of political and philosophical terror in more detail in the next two chapters. However, what is important to bear in mind here is that, for Lyotard, the task of art is to resist the terror of totality through its employment of the sublime.

Instead of discussing art in terms of a reconciliation of knowledge and ethics, then, Lyotard emphasises the disruptions implicit in the *Critique of Judgement*'s analysis of the aesthetic. In 'An Answer to the Question: What is the Postmodern?' he investigates the potential that art has to demonstrate that the world in which we live is discontinuous and not capable of being explained entirely by any rational system. In fact, the point of art for Lyotard is its ability to highlight the failings in such systems.

In the essay, Lyotard distinguishes three types of artistic and cultural presentation: realism, modernism and postmodernism. These terms may well be familiar from the work of other critics. However, it is important to be precise about the way in which Lyotard employs them. In other discussions of postmodernism (see, for example, Hutcheon 1988 or Jameson 1991), the three terms chart a chronological course of artistic development. In this sort of approach, realism is described as the leading aesthetic form of the nineteenth century and is to be found in the works of such writers as George Eliot or Charlotte Brontë, modernism challenges realist representation and leading exponents are novelists like Virginia Woolf or poets like Ezra Pound, and postmodernism is the most recent artistic movement that in its turn challenges the assumptions of modernism and might be discovered in the work of, for example, Thomas Pynchon or Salman Rushdie.

While this way of distinguishing between the three movements might well be helpful in some cases, it is not the distinction that Lyotard deploys in 'An Answer to the Question'. Instead, he presents a more complex picture of art and culture in which realism, modernism and postmodernism coexist simultaneously in all periods of artistic production. So, unlike in *The Postmodern Condition* that describes the postmodern as a late twentieth-century phenomenon, the postmodern in 'An Answer to the Question' is a matter of aesthetic style rather than historical periodisation. Lyotard argues that a work 'can become modern only if it is first postmodern. Thus understood, postmodernism is not modernism at its end, but in a nascent state, and this state is recurrent' (1992: 13). In other words, the postmodern does not replace a worn out modernity, but rather recurs throughout modernity as a nascent state (a state of being born or coming into existence) of modernist transformation. The modern, according to Lyotard, is in a state of constant upheaval because of its continual attempts to innovate and progress. The postmodern is, for Lyotard, an avant-garde force within the upheavals of this modernity that challenges and disrupts its ideas and categories, and makes possible the appearance of new ways of thinking and acting that resist those dominant modern themes of progress and innovation. Thus, for example, it might be possible to describe as postmodern Cervantes' novel, *Don Quixote* (1604) because of the ways in which it shatters the ideas of chivalry and romance that were current in Europe at the end of the medieval period, or Thomas Sterne's *Tristram Shandy* (1761–7) for the way its narrative form destabilises eighteenth-century notions of identity and narrative. In fact, Lyotard goes so far as to argue that Kant's philosophy 'marks at once the prologue and the epilogue of modernity. And as epilogue to modernity, it is also a prologue to postmodernity' (1989: 394), by which he means that Kant's writings stand at the beginning of modernity (and are therefore its prologue) and yet at the same time introduce many of the themes and ideas that will lead to its disruption (thus marking both modernity's epilogue and also an opening of the postmodern within that modernity). This is notion of an imbrication of modernity and the postmodern is quite a complex idea, and to make clear what Lyotard is getting at it is worth working through his definitions of realism, modernism and postmodernism in some detail.

REALISM

For Lyotard, realism is the mainstream art of any culture. It is the art that reflects back a culture's beliefs and ideas in a way that it can immediately recognise. In a later essay, entitled 'A Postmodern Fable', he claims that realism 'is the art of making reality, of knowing reality and knowing how to make reality' (1997: 91). This inverts the standard academic view of realism. Instead of simply reflecting reality through its verisimilitude or, in other words, creating a life-like image of the way the world really is, Lyotard claims that realism 'makes' the world appear to be real. What he is getting at here is that reality is not something that we know naturally, but rather that a sense of reality is generated through the beliefs and ideals of a particular culture, and that realist art or literature is one of the things that helps a culture create a sense of its reality. This is why 'An Answer to the Question' argues that the aim of realist art is to order the world 'from a point of view that would give it recognisable meaning, a syntax and lexicon that would allow addressees [readers or viewers] to decode images and sequences rapidly', and thereby to 'protect consciousness from doubt' (1992: 5–6). For Lyotard, realist art is thus the art we recognise and understand immediately. It presents the world to us in a way that we are used to, and refrains from challenging our beliefs about reality. In other words, realism, by protecting consciousness from doubts about the way things are, serves to perpetuate narratives about the world: the established language games are presented as true or natural and not subject to critique or change.

This realism might well take the form of the styles of narration used in the nineteenth-century novel or the naturalistic performances of actors in many television dramas or soap operas today. However, this is not the full extent of Lyotard's definition: many of the texts and artefacts that are commonly described as postmodern by other critics are also categorised as realist in 'An Answer to the Question'. Lyotard is at pains to distinguish his own account of the postmodern from a common idea about postmodernism, which is that postmodern art is based on eclecticism, irony and the idea that 'anything goes'. For Lyotard, the 'anything goes' idea is not postmodern; rather, it is the realism of contemporary capitalism:

> Eclecticism is the degree zero of contemporary general culture: you listen to reggae; you watch a western; you eat McDonald's at midday and local cuisine at night; you wear Paris perfume in Tokyo and dress retro in Hong Kong; knowledge is the stuff of TV game shows ... Together, artist, gallery owner, critic, and public indulge one another in the Anything Goes – it is time to relax. But this realism of Anything Goes is the realism of money: in the absence of aesthetic criteria it is still possible to measure the value of works of art by the profits they realise.
>
> (1992: 8)

In this scenario of eclecticism, the mixing of different styles, media and cultures is not radical or subversive; rather, it is a function of economic consumption. According to Lyotard this is the day-to-day experience of contemporary culture: the whole world is at one's fingertips so long as one has the cash or credit to consume. Realism, even the realism of the pastiche of 'anything goes', thus adopts the language games of the culture from which it emerges and asserts the stability of those games by reflecting them back to the culture itself.

MODERNISM AND POSTMODERNISM

In contrast to this realism, Lyotard offers two alternatives: modernism and postmodernism, both of which set out to disrupt realism by 'questioning the rules that govern images and narratives'

(1992: 12). These are not two entirely different aesthetic or historical forms. Rather, the postmodern is a modification of the modern that further radicalises the latter's challenges to realist representation. Lyotard defines modernism as

> the art that devotes its 'trivial technique', as Diderot called it, to presenting the existence of something unpresentable. Showing that there is something we can conceive of which we can neither see nor show – this is the stake of modern painting.
>
> (1992: 11)

The idea of presenting the fact that there is something unpresentable is a key idea in Lyotard's thought, and one that has frequently been misunderstood. Because it is so important for his definitions of both modernism and postmodernism it is crucial to grasp what might be at stake in it. Lyotard derives the idea of presenting that there is an unpresentable from Kant's discussion of the sublime.

THE SUBLIME

The term 'sublime' originates in classical philosophy. However, during the eighteenth century, with the rise of aesthetics, the sublime became a subject of debate and controversy. For Lyotard, the most important account of sublimity is found in the work of Immanuel Kant. In the *Critique of Judgement*, Kant distinguishes two forms of aesthetic experience: the beautiful and the sublime. Both of these are feelings that occur when one comes in contact with an object (whether it is a painting or poem, or a seascape or starry sky). Beauty is a feeling of harmony between oneself and that object: it appears perfectly shaped for one's perception and generates a sense of well being. With the sublime, the response is more complex. One is simultaneously attracted and repelled by the object, enthralled by it and also horrified.

For Kant, a feeling of the sublime occurs when one comes face to face with something too large or powerful to represent adequately to oneself. Kant argues that the imagination is stretched to the limit trying to represent what is perceived and one feels pain. This pain, however, is simultaneously pleasurable: the disappointment of not being able to adequately picture what is perceived is accompanied by the feeling of pleasure at being able to conceive it. In this sense, it indicates through feeling that there is something beyond the 'limits of experience' that we can conceive of even if we can't represent or know it. *What* causes the sublime feeling is unpresentable, but within that feeling it is possible to conceive *that* there is something. Hence Lyotard's formulation of the sublime: 'presenting the existence of something unpresentable'.

Lyotard adopts the idea of the sublime to describe the way in which art or literature can disrupt established language games and ways of representing the world. Modern art, he argues, has the capacity to present the fact that the unpresentable exists: that there are things that are impossible to present in available language games, voices that are silenced in culture, ideas that cannot be formulated in rational communication.

Following the two parts of the sublime feeling (pain and pleasure), the existence of the unpresentable can be signalled by the sublime in two distinct ways, one of which Lyotard calls modern and the other postmodern. This difference is the basis of the distinction between the two forms. Lyotard describes this difference in terms of modernist nostalgia and postmodern jubilation:

The accent can fall on the inadequacy of the faculty of presentation, on the nostalgia for presence experienced by the human subject and the obscure and futile will that animates it in spite of everything. Or else the accent can fall on the power of the faculty to conceive, on what one might call its 'inhumanity' . . . and on the extension of being and

jubilation that come from inventing new rules of the game, whether
pictorial, artistic, or something else.

(1992: 13)

The modernist sublime is thus tied up with the feeling of loss: the
old language games no longer present the world adequately, and
the feeling evoked is a wish to return to the stability of that earlier
state. On the other hand, the postmodern sublime works through a
sense of excitement at the failure of language games: 'the old rules
have failed', it announces, 'let us discover new ones'. In this sense,
conception runs ahead of presentation, as the collapsing structure of
the realism challenged by the work of art indicates the possibility
of a new, different, 'inhuman' way of experiencing and thinking
about the world.

Helpfully, Lyotard provides a clear example of the distinction
between modernism and postmodernism, each of which he argues
'allude to something that does not let itself be made present' (1992:
13). On the side of modernism, he places *A la recherche du temps perdu*
(1913–27), the novel by the French writer Marcel Proust (1871–
1922) that has been translated into English as both *Remembrance of
Things Past* and, more recently, *In Search of Lost Time*. Proust's novel
is one about memory and time. Its narrative is continually spurred on
by the recurrence of memories evoked by stimuli, such as eating a
madeline or tripping on a paving stone, which constantly promise to
reveal and shape the character of the narrator. According to Lyotard,
'the thing that is eluded . . . is the identity of consciousness, falling
prey to an excess of time' (1992: 14). In other words, the true character of the narrator remains finally unpresentable. However, despite
this gap in presentation, the narrative itself retains a traditional form
that presents the story as a unified whole. For Lyotard, this makes
Proust's work nostalgic, and therefore modern: 'it allows the unpresentable to be invoked only as absent content, while form, thanks
to its recognisable consistency, continues to offer the reader or
spectator material for consolation and pleasure' (1992: 14).

In contrast to this, Lyotard cites the later work of the Irish novelist James Joyce (1882–1941) as postmodern. In novels such as *Ulysses* (1922) and *Finnegans Wake* (1939), Lyotard argues that 'Joyce makes us discern the unpresentable in the writing itself . . . A whole range of accepted narrative and even stylistic operators is brought into play with no concern for the unity of the whole, and experiments are conducted with new operators' (1992: 14). In other words, the sublime in Joyce is not just a question of missing contents such as the identity of the narrator, but rather occurs in the writing itself. Joyce's use of puns, obscure allusions, quotations and his disruptions of the established ideas of linear development and narrative sense, challenge the reader's presuppositions about what a novel should be and continually undermine the desire to make the work make sense. One might constantly be at a loss about what the novel is about, but that loss is itself enjoyable and stimulating, and might just lead one to raise questions about one's everyday sense-making processes.

Lyotard's discussion of Joyce leads to his clearest definition of postmodern aesthetics:

> The postmodern would be that which in the modern invokes the unpresentable in presentation itself, that which refuses the consolation of correct forms, refuses the consensus of taste permitting a common experience of nostalgia for the impossible, and inquires into new presentations – not to take pleasure in them, but to better produce the feeling that there is something unpresentable.
>
> (1992: 15)

For Lyotard then, postmodern art disrupts established artistic structures and language games by testifying to the existence of the unpresentable, not as something missing from the content of a work but as a force that shatters traditional ways of narrating or representing. Postmodern works are disorienting: they break the rules and undermine the categories that the reader or viewer are used to, and raise the questions of 'what is art?' and 'what is reality?' in their very structure.

Unlike Habermas' notion of art as a way of generating reconciliation, then, for Lyotard art's potential to disorient, disrupt and challenge is the key to its importance. Postmodern art, he says must wage a 'war on totality' (1992: 16) by testifying to the unpresentable. This potential to challenge established language games and totalities gives art a key role in thought, ethics and politics, as the next chapter will demonstrate.

SUMMARY

Lyotard's 'An Answer to the Question: What is the Postmodern?' opens questions about the role of art and aesthetics in the post-modern. In this essay, Lyotard explores the importance of Immanuel Kant's account of the sublime for thinking about the potential that art might have to disrupt established language games. Because the sublime can 'present the fact that something remains unpresentable' in these language games, it can point to new possibilities for thought and action. In contrast to Jürgen Habermas, who argues that the strength of art is that it has the potential to present a reconciliation between the language games of truth and justice, Lyotard sees art's role as shattering people's common-sense understandings of the way the world works. He argues that realist art serves to reassure this common sense, but that modern and postmodern art employ the sublime to demonstrate understanding's limits and point to new possibilities. For Lyotard, the postmodern is a radicalisation of the modern. In the modern, the sublime appears through the missing contents of a work, whereas the postmodern sublime enacts a disruption not only of the contents but also of the formal mode of presentation itself.

3

PHRASES AND THE DIFFEREND: LYOTARD'S POLITICS

The last two chapters began to describe the ways in which Lyotard's idea of the postmodern sets out to challenge established ways of thinking about and viewing the world and 'reality'. The question that arises from this is how these challenges produce action. How, in other words, do the paralogical disruptions of scientific language games and the sublime disturbances of aesthetic presentation lead to a different idea of ethics and politics?

While neither *The Postmodern Condition* nor 'An Answer to the Question: What is the Postmodern?' excludes ethical or political questions (indeed, both are intensely concerned with them), the aim of this chapter is to examine more closely the frameworks for action that arise from Lyotard's thought. It will do so through readings of two texts that he was working on at around the same time as *The Postmodern Condition*, both of which take up many of the themes and ideas introduced there and focus them on issues of justice and politics. These texts have been translated into English as *Just Gaming* (1985) and *The Differend: Phrases in Dispute* (1988). The key question that guides this chapter is thus: what sort of ethical or political theory is possible in the light of the postmodern collapse of metanarrative legitimation? In answering this question, this chapter will outline the structures Lyotard employs to ask political and philosophical questions about history, art and criticism (which will be discussed in more detail in the next three chapters).

JUST GAMING

Just Gaming takes the form of a series of dialogues conducted over seven different 'days' (which actually took place over seven months between November 1977 and June 1978) between Lyotard and Jean-Loup Thébaud, the editor of a French journal called *L'esprit*. Thébaud questions Lyotard about the political and ethical implications of his philosophy, and pushes him to define what he sees as the basis for justice in the light of the collapse of the metanarratives.

On the second day of the discussion, Lyotard presents one of his clearest formulations about the relation between politics and ethics:

> When one says politics, one always insists that there is something to institute. There is no politics if there is not at the very centre of society, at least at a centre that is not a centre but everywhere in the society, a questioning of existing institutions, a project to improve them, to make them more just. This means that all politics implies the prescription of doing something else than what is.
>
> (1985: 23)

Politics is active: it is the attempt to question and improve the society in which one lives, to change what is. And yet, for Lyotard, this questioning and improving is tied to the question of the 'just'. He argues that politics implies and emerges from what he calls a 'prescription'. A prescription is a type of language game that is different from denotation. This difference is crucial for Lyotard. Denotation is the language game that functions in the realm of knowledge: a denotative statement points to or describes something; for example, 'the chair is comfortable' denotes a state of affairs that pertain to a chair

– the fact that the utterer of the statement finds it comfortable. A prescriptive statement is part of a different language game: it does not describe a state of affairs but aims to bring one about. Examples of this might be a request such as 'Please close the door' or an order such as 'Off with his head!'. In both of these cases, there is no explicit description of how the world actually is (although the door's being open or the man's head still being on is implied), but rather a call to bring about the required state (the door being closed or the man's head being removed from his shoulders). In other words, denotation describes the world and prescription attempts to change it. For Lyotard, this difference between denotation and prescription is the basis for thinking about politics and justice.

Lyotard argues that it is ethically vital to take account of the difference between denotation and prescription. In this he follows Kant who, as the last chapter argued, drew a division between epistemology and ethics, between the 'is' and the 'ought'. In philosophy, this division is called the 'fact–value distinction'.

THE FACT–VALUE DISTINCTION

The fact–value distinction remains the subject of much controversy in philosophy. Briefly described, proponents of this distinction argue that while facts denote actual states of affairs in the world ('The sea is wet', for example), values emerge from human relations and subjective propensities (such as, 'swimming in the sea is pleasurable') and are therefore of a different order. Perhaps the most famous formulation of this distinction occurs in a book by the Scottish Enlightenment philosopher, David Hume (1711–76), called *A Treatise on Human Nature* (1739–40). Hume argues that conclusions about 'ought' ('You ought to do this or that') cannot logically be derived from facts about 'is', but rest on other premises such as a subjective propensity about what is desirable or a cultural consensus about what is permissible. This is usually formulated as 'you can't get an "ought" from an "is"'.

In other words, the way a given state of affairs 'is' doesn't logically determine how we 'ought' to respond to it; rather, the value of a response must be derived from other criteria. Kant's abyss between epistemology and ethics is another key example of this distinction.

Lyotard observes the importance of the fact–value distinction, and argues that the sort of politics that ignores it, that bases its prescriptions on the belief that values naturally spring from a true state of affairs, can lead to totalitarianism. He argues that there are two ways in which modern politics can do this, which bear similarities to the types of grand narrative that are outlined in *The Postmodern Condition*.

The first way of reducing the distinction between prescription and denotation is to base the former on the latter, after the manner of the speculative grand narrative. It emerges from

> the deep conviction that there is a true being of society, and that society will be just if it is brought into conformity with this true being, and therefore one can draw just prescriptions from a description that is true, in the sense of 'correct'. The passage from the true to the just is a passage that is the *If, then*.
>
> (1985: 23)

In this idea of politics, knowledge about the way the world or a society really is produces its own form of justice from the truth of its descriptions. The just becomes part of the true, and the idea of a 'good society' that is developed implies specific ways of acting ethically. This 'good society' is an object of knowledge that sets out, in a series of denotative statements, a theory of what will make life perfect. Ethics is then based on propositions such as '*If* the good society is X, *then* we should do Y'. The problem here is that the true, and therefore the just, is handed down by an authority that determines for the people the way they should live, generating a system that remains beyond question for them. Examples of this might be religious societies that found their laws on assumptions about the will of a god or gods, or societies based on a specific philosophy such as Communism that has a particular view of what the world is and controls its people in order to make it that way: 'if the Bible tells us that the good society is Christian, then all non-believers should be converted' or 'if the Communist Party says that society should be based on equality, then we should abolish privilege and private property'. In other words, this sort of society is fundamentalist: the truth of goodness is given in advance and the people must conform to it or be punished.

The second problematic form of justice relates more closely to the grand narrative of emancipation. In this formulation, justice is based on an idea of the general will of the people who form an 'autonomous group',

> a group that believes that justice lies in the self-determination of peoples. In other words, there is a close relation between autonomy and self-determination: one gives oneself one's own laws.
>
> (1985: 31)

In this model, prescriptions are not handed down from above but are inhabited by the people: for example, 'I am American, and there-fore I believe in the American way of life'. This is the basis of a democratic model of society in which everyone has a stake in its laws to the extent that they identify themselves with that society, believe in its ideals, vote in its elections, etc. However, Lyotard claims this model too can lead to its own form of totalitarianism based on a form of imperialism. As Bill Readings argues, 'totalitarianism is evident when a society claims to have embodied justice, to represent the law, so that it is able to dismiss any criticism of itself as simply "un-American" or "anti-soviet" or "counter-revolutionary"' (Readings 1991: 111). The identification of the just with the will of the people allows that people to pass judgement on foreigners or those within their society who don't hold its ideals on the basis of laws those others may not recognise. One only needs to recall the many wars fought on the basis of social ideals such as the European crusades against the 'heathens' during the Middle Ages, or the persecution of suspected communists in the United States in the 1950s. In both cases the ideals of a particular people were determined as the most free and just, and those that did not share them were suppressed.

With the destruction of metanarratives in postmodern thought, Lyotard claims, these two models can no longer gain theoretical support and their potential for injustice becomes more evident. In contrast, he presents a notion of ethics that tries to avoid reducing the just to the true or to the will of a particular group 'that is author-ised to say "we"' (1985: 81). He argues that prescriptive language games are irreducible to denotative ones, meaning that justice is not simply a question of making or obeying a set of laws but, rather, consists of being open to the differences between language games, and the fact they are not reducible to a single metalanguage. For this reason, like the Kantian categorical imperative, Lyotard's notion of justice can 'have no content . . . we have to judge case by case' (1985: 47). In other words, empirical laws such as 'Thou shalt not kill' do not make sense as ethical universals because they are always subject to exceptions: what about in a 'just' war or in self-defence, both of which are condoned in the very text that presents this law (see 1985: 63–72)? For Lyotard, justice is based on recognition of the hetero-geneity of people and language games, and respect for the individu-ality of each one – which would itself mitigate against murder or any other form of elimination of the other's difference. Injustice occurs in the exclusion or silencing of particular people or languages:

> Absolute injustice would occur if . . . the possibility of continuing to play the game of the just were excluded. That is what is unjust. Not the opposite of the just, but that which prohibits that the question of the just and the unjust be, and remain, raised. Thus, obviously, all terror, annihilation, massacre, etc., or their threat, are by definition, unjust . . . But moreover, any decision that takes away, or in which it happens that

Injustice excludes someone from making statements about the just, whether by killing them or by forbidding their voice from being heard. To be just is to allow others to participate in the 'game of the just', to respect their difference and allow them to speak for themselves. This seems relatively straightforward, but the implications of Lyotard's position are complex and far reaching in the way they point towards a new conception of politics. This new conception is introduced in *Just Gaming*, but is more thoroughly developed in Lyotard's most philosophically rigorous book, *The Differend*.

Before moving on to discuss *The Differend*, however, I want to introduce a short narrative that opens up a problem of justice of the type that will be crucial to Lyotard arguments in that book.

THE LAND DISPUTE

Imagine that you are an Australian judge (this story is based on a series of events that have happened recently in Australian courts – see Gelder and Jacobs 1998: 117–34). Before you are two plaintiffs. The first is a construction company who want to build a new development on an island; the second is a group of aboriginal women who claim that the island is a religious site for their community. If what the women say is true then the development, which has already cost the company many thousands of dollars, must be scrapped and the land returned. This, the company tell you, will probably bankrupt them and force them to make their staff redundant.

In order to substantiate their claim, the women must prove in court that the island really is a holy site. But this is where the problem arises. You are told by the women's lawyer that, according to their beliefs, they can only discuss the meaning of the site amongst themselves: the site's holiness rests on the belief that it remains a secret passed down from mother to daughter along the generations, and if this secret is revealed to a man or to anyone outside their group then the site loses its holiness. They are thus trapped. According to the law, if they don't provide evidence in court then they lose the case; if they do speak out then they must reveal the secret, which means that the site loses its holiness in their eyes and, again, they lose the case.

This is the problem with which you, as the judge, are faced. You have no possible way of knowing whether or not the women are telling the truth, as they cannot give evidence in court. On the one hand, there is the possibility that you will wrong the women by allowing a place that is sacred to them be destroyed. On the other hand, you run the risk of bankrupting a company and making its workers redundant. What do you do?

THE DIFFEREND: PHRASES IN DISPUTE

Lyotard himself acknowledges that *The Differend* is his most complex and philosophical book. He began work on it in 1974, and took nine years to complete it (it was first published in French in 1983), during which time he also wrote both *The Postmodern Condition* and *Just Gaming*. *The Differend* picks up on and develops many of the ideas in these two earlier texts, and goes much further than them in thinking about contemporary knowledge, ethics, art and politics. In fact, some critics have claimed that the two earlier texts are little more than rehearsals of arguments that are fully developed in *The Differend* (see, for example, Bennington 1988 and Williams 2000).

Like the other texts that have been introduced, the form of *The Differend* is important to notice. It opens with a brief summary and outline of the argument called a 'Reading Dossier' that sets out what is at stake in the book as well as the methodology employed. The main part of the text is made up of a series of 264 numbered paragraphs that lay out Lyotard's argument in detail. These paragraphs are interspersed with 'notices' that discuss particular ideas, writers and texts (such as Kant, Hegel, the Cashinahua, etc.) whose arguments are germane to development of Lyotard's case. Because of the fragmentary nature of the text, it is left to the reader to forge the links between the different paragraphs and notices – and, as we shall see, the problem of linkage is crucial to what *The Differend* is about. The rest of this chapter will introduce *The Differend* and show how its arguments expand on those in the earlier books, and the next three chapters will begin to draw out some of the implications of its arguments for postmodern art, culture, criticism and politics.

The Differend begins with a series of examples similar to the story told in the last section (the most important of which, the possibility of testifying to the reality of the Holocaust, will be discussed in the next chapter) that point to a moment where what Lyotard refers to as a 'wrong' occurs:

> This is what a wrong would be: a damage accompanied by the loss of the means to prove the damage. This is the case if the victim is deprived of life, or of all his or her liberties, or of the freedom to make his or her ideas or opinions public, or simply the right to testify to the damage, or even more simply if the testifying phrase is itself deprived of authority . . . In all of these cases, to the privation constituted by the damage there is added the impossibility of bringing it to the knowledge of others, and in particular the knowledge of the tribunal.
>
> (1988a: 5)

This passage reformulates Lyotard's conclusions about 'absolute injustice' in *Just Gaming*. To work from the perspective of the aboriginal women in the example, the 'damage' would be the threat to their land by the developer and, more importantly here, the 'wrong' emerges from their inability to testify in court to the truth of that damage. If they tell the truth they lose their land (because, by revealing the secret, it ceases to have value for them), but if they remain silent they must lose the case and, therefore, their land. They are thus prevented from 'playing the game of the just'.

Because there is no way for them to present evidence, the women (and also the developer) are caught up in what Lyotard calls a differend:

> As distinguished from a litigation, a differend would be a case of conflict, between (at least) two parties, that cannot be resolved for lack of a rule of judgement applicable to both of the arguments. One side's legitimacy does not imply the other's lack of legitimacy. However, applying a single rule of judgement to both in order to settle their differend as though it were merely a litigation would wrong (at least) one of them (and both of them if neither side admits this rule).
>
> (1988a: xi)

Between the women and the developer is a differend that, within the rules of the legal system (a language game in Lyotard's sense in *Just Gaming*), cannot be resolved without wronging one side or the other. Either the judge finds against the women because their evidence is lacking (or self-defeating if they speak) or he finds against the developer by changing the rules part way through the legal game. Returning to the categories of *The Postmodern Condition* for a moment, the judge does not have access to a metalanguage that can impartially decide between the different languages that each side uses. In fact, in *The Differend*, no such impartial metalanguage is ever possible. Any legal decision made by the judge will necessarily wrong one or both of the plaintiffs because they cannot adduce the same sorts of proof to support their claims. According to Lyotard, then, a differend 'is signalled by this inability to prove. The one who lodges a complaint is heard, but the one who is the victim [of a wrong], and who is perhaps the same one, is reduced to silence' (1988a: 10). The women, put in an impossible situation before the court, are reduced to silence and become victims of the judicial system; or, if the judge decides in their favour, the developers are wronged because the court has employed rules that are different from those established in law to find against them.

Differends are not simply a matter of legal dispute, however. More generally, Lyotard describes a differend as 'the unstable state of language wherein something which must be able to be put into phrases cannot yet be' (1988a: 13). The differend is a moment of silence, a stutter in the flow of language, where the right words will not come. It marks a point of suffering where an injustice cannot find a space to make itself heard, where an injury is silenced and becomes a wrong. And, Lyotard claims, these differends are far more common than one might at first suppose. In the terms that he employed in *Just Gaming*, a differend occurs when one language game imposes its rules and values on another and prevents it from retaining its own, autonomous way of speaking. All that remains is a feeling of injustice and wrong.

Differends are the point of departure for Lyotard's exploration of the politics and philosophy of language in *The Differend*. He argues that the aim of thought must be to try to

> find new rules for forming and linking phrases that are able to express the differend disclosed by the feeling [of injustice], unless one wants the differend to be smothered right away in a litigation and for the alarm sounded by the feeling to have been useless.
>
> (1988a: 13)

In order to investigate the implications for thinking that the differend throws up, Lyotard produces a more complex and powerful theory of language than that proposed in the idea of language games employed in *The Postmodern Condition* and *Just Gaming*, which is based on the term that has cropped up in some of the preceding quotations: the phrase.

PHRASES, PHRASE REGIMENS AND GENRES OF DISCOURSE

Lyotard recasts language games as phrases to avoid two possible confusions that may have arisen from his earlier work. First, despite his numerous claims to the contrary, the notion of a language game suggests that subjects exist outside them as 'players'; and, second, the term 'language game' is imprecise in that it refers both to types of statement such as denotation or prescription and also to the ways in which these statements are linked together to form discourses such as science, narrative or politics. Showing how his use of a theory of phrases overcomes these problems should serve to make clear what Lyotard means by the term 'phrase'.

Lyotard moves from the notion of language games to that of phrases firstly in order to 'refute the prejudice anchored in the reader by centuries of humanism and of "human sciences" that there is "man", that there is "language", that the former makes use of the latter for his own ends' (1988a: xiii).

HUMANISM

Humanism emerged as a cultural, philosophical and literary movement in the second half of the fourteenth century. Its rapid spread and frequent transformation during the Renaissance and subsequent centuries makes a straightforward or exhaustive definition all but impossible. However, one might locate its essential ingredient as being recognition of the value, dignity and centrality of the individual human being who is seen as the source of reason, knowledge and action. At its beginnings, humanism marked the enlightenment idea of the emancipation of 'Man' from religious or spiritual mysticism. In more recent times, humanism has been associated with almost all of modernity's grand narratives, from Christian humanism to Marxist and existential humanisms. For a detailed account of the history and complexities of humanism, and for its relation to literary and cultural studies, see Tony Davis' introductory book, *Humanism* (1997).

Humanism, however, is only one way of thinking about reality (and not, for Lyotard, the most persuasive). He argues that the phrase is a more direct point of departure since 'it is immediately presupposed' (1988a: xi) in even the humanist's sense of 'I think' or 'I am' as each is itself a phrase. Who or what the human being is always has to be defined, whether through biology, psychology, theology or philosophy, and this will always be done in phrases.

A phrase is not simply something that is said by someone, although it can be that. It is any case of the transfer of information of any sort. So, for example, it may be a piece of speech or writing, but it might also be a laugh or a scream, an animal cry or the shape 'presented by the tail of a cat' (1988a: 140). Lyotard argues that even 'silence makes a phrase' (1988a: ix): a refusal or inability to speak or respond means something. A phrase brings together four points each time it occurs: the 'addressor' who presents the phrase, the 'addressee' to whom the phrase is presented, the 'reference' that the phrase is about, and the 'sense' which is what the phrase says about the reference. These four instances make up the 'phrase universe', which 'consists in the situating of these instances in relation to each other' (1988a: 14). In other words, if we take the phrase 'The cat is white', the addressor is the one who speaks it, the addressee is the person or people to whom it is spoken, the referent is the cat and the sense is that the referent 'is white'. Each instance is brought into relation by the phrase to form a particular 'universe'. None of the four instances pre-exists the phrase or is its origin; rather, each comes into existence as an instance as the phrase happens. From this point of view, subjects, meanings and referents come into being as effects of the relation between phrases.

What becomes the focus of Lyotard's argument is the way in which phrases are linked to each other. He argues that it is necessary to link on to a phrase: one responds to it even if one remains silent or ignores it (both of which would themselves be phrases). However, the type of response is contingent, as it is possible to respond to any given phrase in a myriad of ways. In response to the phrase 'the cat is white', for example, the addressee might say 'yes, it is', 'it looks black to me', 'that isn't a cat, it's a dog', or even

'I love the sound of your voice when you say that'. Each of these linkages implies very different things: consent, argument about the sense (the cat's whiteness), disagreement about the referent (it is a dog rather than a cat), or even a change of referent from the cat to the voice of the addressor of the first phrase. There has to be a link, but different ways of linking take the exchange in very different directions.

In discussing this question of linking phrases, Lyotard resolves another difficulty with the imprecision of language games – the fact that the category 'language game' is too general and unspecific because it refers both to types of language such as denotation and prescription, and also to more general discourses such as science, ethics or literature. In *The Differend*, he distinguishes between what he calls 'phrase regimens', which refer to the former, and 'genres of discourse' that include the latter. The different regimens, which would include denoting, prescribing, showing, asking, describing, reasoning, ordering, etc., are all different ways of relating the four instances of the phrase universe. Different regimens would thus present different sets of relations between the four instances that are marked in a phrase: for example, the relationship between the addressor and addressee would be different in an order from those that obtain in a request, or the relations between sense and reference would be different in a question from those in a denotation. This means, Lyotard claims, that phrases 'obeying different regimens are untranslatable into one another' (1988a: 48). This is a more general version of the argument in *Just Gaming* about facts and values: each regimen forms phrases differently, and it is thus impossible for phrase in one regimen to be the same if it occurs in another.

Genres of discourse are different from phrase regimens, and are ways of organising the relationships between them. Genres, Lyotard argues, 'fix the rules of linkage . . . determine the stakes, they submit phrases from different regimens to a single finality' (1988a: 29). In other words, a particular genre such as science might employ phrases from a number of regimens such as questioning, describing, defining, proving, reasoning, etc., in order to achieve a particular end: to obtain an accurate description of the workings of nature, for example. Another genre, such as literature, might employ phrases from the same regimens, but its end would be different: to create new visions of the world in which we live, perhaps. Different genres of discourse have different criteria for judging the value of particular ways of linking onto phrases, and each genre would forbid certain forms of linking. In science, for instance, it would not be legitimate to link the phrase 'Isn't that pretty!' to 'Copper sulphate in a solid state consists of blue crystals', as to do so would immediately take one outside of the discourse of science and into aesthetics. A genre of discourse is thus a means of giving validity to certain forms of linkage and organising phrases into a body of knowledge.

A phrase therefore carries with it a great deal more information than just what it signifies: by relating the four instances, fitting into a regimen and being focused towards an end by a genre, the phrase opens up a universe of social relationships. So, for example, the phrase 'long live the king' obviously tells us of the addressor's (not necessarily genuine) desire that the monarch survive for an extended time. However, its conventional nature (fitting into a genre of state ceremony), the relation that obtains between whoever the addressor and addressee are (is it spoken by a noble to coerce her or his servants to conform or a peasant trying to get the monarch's attention in order to present a petition), or the phrases that are permitted to be linked to it by the genre in which it occurs, all open up a range of other possibilities for analysis.

According to Lyotard, phrases are immediately social: 'The social is always presupposed because it is presented or copresented with the slightest phrase' (1988a: 139). Moreover, because of the necessity of linking on to any given phrase with another phrase (even a silence), the question of *what* phrase to respond with is, for Lyotard, always political. It is thus that he opens up a sense of politics in *The Differend*.

PHRASES, POLITICS AND THE SOCIAL

For Lyotard, politics is not simply one genre of discourse among others. Rather, it emerges in every decision about how to link on to a phrase. These decisions take place within genres and are thus tied up with a particular genre's rules for linking and its aims. Lyotard argues that, a genre of discourse 'imposes its mode of linking onto "our" phrase and onto "us" . . . This conflict is a differend, since the success (or the validation) proper to one genre is not proper to others' (1988a: 136). Every time a particular link is made, all other possible links (the links that are not permitted by the genre within which one is operating) are silenced. Although there will always be a myriad of possible linkages, a myriad of responses, only one can actually occur. This 'turns every linkage into a kind of "victory" of one [genre] over the others. These others remain neglected, forgotten, or repressed responsibilities' (1988a: 136). On deciding in favour of either the women or the developer in the land rights example introduced earlier, the judge must fix on a particular judgment phrase that refuses all other possible judgments.

This 'victory' of one phrase over other possible phrases in every linkage is the basis for a politics of the differend, which is a notion of politics that emerges in every action or phrase:

> Politics . . . is the threat of the differend. It is not a genre, it is the multiplicity of genres, the diversity of ends, and par excellence the question of linkage . . . Everything is political if politics is the possibility of the differend on the occasion of the slightest linkage.
>
> (1988a: 138–9)

Every linkage is political as it is based on the decision of one form of linking (genre of discourse) over the others. In every linkage, all of the other possibilities are refused or repressed, and the potential emergence of other voices is denied.

The question of the political, at its most fundamental level, thus arises everywhere: there is no decision, action, occurrence or text that is not in some way political as it is tied up with the differend. In many cases, the stakes of this politics might appear trivial, but in others the implications of a single phrase can transform lives, cultures and the movement of the world. To return to the example of the land dispute, the way in which the women decide to link on to the phrase demanding evidence entails a political decision (whether to speak or remain silent). Equally, how the judge decides to respond to the women's phrase has immense ramifications, not just for the particular case but also for the Australian legal system and society as a whole. The judge may either ignore the differend between the two parties and continue to work within the legal genre (thereby almost certainly finding against the women) or respond to their differend and begin to search for new means of reaching a just resolution to their dispute by attempting to transform the genre in which it has hitherto been phrased.

The ethical role of the thinker, according to Lyotard, is to uncover the moments where a differend has occurred and something has been silenced, and to find ways to make what has been deprived of a voice heard: 'One's responsibility before thought consists . . . in detecting differends and in finding the (impossible) idiom for phrasing them' (1988a: 142). This is not simply a question of settling differends by resorting to a universal genre with rules applicable to all the parties (as such a genre is, according to Lyotard, not available). Rather, it is a case of affirming or attesting to the existence of the differend and searching for new modes and idioms in which to phrase the dispute. This, Lyotard argues, is the role of the postmodern thinker: 'What is at stake in a literature, in a philosophy, in a politics perhaps, is to bear witness to differends by finding idioms for them' (1988a: 13). Quite how important this task is, and how it can be achieved, will be the subjects of the next three chapters.

SUMMARY

Lyotard is first and foremost a political thinker, and this inflects all of his readings of art, literature and culture. His book, *Just Gaming*, investigates the possibility of thinking about justice in the wake of the collapse of the grand narratives. Lyotard follows the Kantian distinction between facts and values, and argues for the danger of basing ethical decisions on ideas about the reality of states of affairs. Instead, Lyotard proposes a system of ethics based on the recognition of others' rights to employ their own language games (and hence values) to present their points of view. Injustice occurs when other ways of thinking, speaking and acting are silenced by the language games of a dominant group or culture.

The Differend is Lyotard's most important work. Here he develops a more complex conception of language based on the idea of the 'phrase'. The focus of the book's analysis becomes the question of how phrases can be linked together and what the implications of different linkages might be. Phrases, according to Lyotard, are categorised into regimens (such as denotation, questioning or ordering, for example), and genres of discourse (such as science, literature, Marxism, etc.) generate sets of principles by which types of linkage between phrases are judged as good or bad. The conflict between different genres is the space in which political decisions are made as one chooses between the different possibilities for phrasing they permit and the silences they impose. Lyotard argues that each time one phrase is linked to another there is the possibility of a differend occurring. He defines a differend as a moment at which one side or other in a conflict is placed in a position where it is impossible to phrase, and argues that it is these differends that mark the points at which criticism should begin.

4

HISTORY, POLITICS AND REPRESENTATION

The last chapter introduced Lyotard's notion of the differend, which plays a central role in his later thought. As an illustration of the implications of the problem that Lyotard seeks to address with it, the chapter narrated the story of a court case between a group of Aboriginal women and a land developer. This is not Lyotard's own example, however. What this chapter will do is investigate Lyotard's key instance of a differend in order to examine some of the consequences he draws from it for thinking about politics and history. Through this discussion it will both expand upon the theory of a politics of the differend, and also explain the relation that Lyotard constructs between history, grand narratives and the postmodern.

THE DIFFEREND OF AUSCHWITZ

Auschwitz, the Nazi concentration camp in which many thousands of Jews were slaughtered during the Second World War, marks, for Lyotard, a moment in which much of the history and thought of Western civilisation founders. It is, for this reason, a key to his thinking about contemporary politics in *The Differend*. The question

he asks is, if Auschwitz marks a point of absolute barbaric ir-
rationality, how can we think it? What does Auschwitz do to thought,
history and politics? What sorts of history, thought and politics are
possible in the aftermath of Auschwitz?

Lyotard's analysis of this question in *The Differend* begins not with
Auschwitz itself, however, but with the arguments put forward by
a French revisionist historian, Robert Faurisson, who seeks to deny
that the Holocaust ever took place. In a piece of deliberately twisted
logic Faurisson claims that the only proof he will accept for the existence of gas chambers in Nazi Germany is the testimony of someone
who has 'seen one with his own eyes'. In other words, only somebody who has been through a gas chamber while it was in operation
and survived will, for Faurisson, be capable of testifying to its reality.
Lyotard points out the obvious impossibility of Faurisson's request
for such a witness:

> His argument is: in order for a place to be identified as a gas chamber,
> the only eyewitness I will accept would be a victim of this gas chamber;
> now, according to my opponent, there is no victim that is not dead; other-
> wise this gas chamber would not be what he or she claims it to be. There
> is, therefore, no gas chamber.
>
> (1988a: 3–4)

In other words, for Faurisson's viciously twisted logic, the only
acceptable proof for the reality of the gas chambers is the testimony
of someone who has been through one and survived. And yet even
this proof would immediately falsify the claims about the Holocaust
as if there were a survivor of a gas chamber then the chambers
couldn't have been as murderous as is popularly supposed. The
Holocaust survivor is thus placed in the position where testimony is
impossible: he or she is silenced by Faurisson's genre of discourse
and falls prey to a differend.

Focusing on the denial of the Holocaust by a revisionist historian
is a very odd beginning to a book on politics. Why does Lyotard give

space to such absurd claims and appear to think they are worth responding to? There is substantial documentary evidence of the reality of the Holocaust, and the arguments of those who seek to deny it have rightly been shown again and again to be false and fraudulent. So what is Lyotard trying to achieve by replaying this argument?

First, the discussion of Faurisson acts as a provocation: it shocks the reader and implicates her or him in the question of how to respond to the politics of the ultra-right by invoking an argument that clearly seeks to deny a commonly held view of reality. It also demonstrates the ability of genres of discourse to silence arguments, and raises the question of whether more commonly followed genres might also have the same effect. More importantly, though, it allows Lyotard to raise a series of questions about the ethics and politics of history writing in general. There is no question that Lyotard gives any credence to Faurisson's position, but his discussion of it brings to light some of the potential shortcomings of an approach to Auschwitz from the perspective of a traditional account of history. Lyotard argues that,

> Millions of human beings were exterminated. Many of the means to prove the crime or its quality were also exterminated . . . What could be established by historical inquiry would be the quantity of the crime. But the documents necessary for the validation were themselves destroyed in quantity . . . The result is that one cannot adduce numerical proof of the massacre and that a historian pleading for the trial's revision will be able to object at great length that the crime has not been established in its quantity.
>
> (1988a: 56)

According to Lyotard, the forms of history based on the organisation of statistical and empirical evidence about the Holocaust will always find it impossible to provide a complete account because so many of the documents and witnesses were systematically destroyed – and that this is in itself a part of what makes the Holocaust unique. The historian's account will necessarily be incomplete, and the revisionist will thus be able to pounce on the gaps to argue for its untruth.

A number of critics (see, for example, Norris 1999 and Browning 2000) have complained, perhaps with some justification, that Lyotard overplays the difficulty here: historians have a range of resources for establishing the credibility of their accounts of the Holocaust. Besides, historical evidence is always necessarily partial, and historians are trained to cope with that. However, this is not entirely what is at stake – Lyotard is making a more complex and far-ranging point than just that there might be evidence missing or destroyed. The genre of history, he argues, tends to treat the Holocaust just like any other historical event to be explained and quantitatively evaluated if it sticks to the discourse of empirical evidence. And yet, according to Lyotard, 'with Auschwitz, something new has happened in history' (1988a: 57), which is the systematic and technological imposition of a differend upon a whole people: not only was there an attempt to exterminate the Jews, but also the whole bureaucratic apparatus of the Nazi state was employed to silence any possibility of their testifying to the injuries they suffered. Consequently,

> The shades of those to whom had been refused not only life but also the expression of the wrong done to them by the Final Solution continue to wander in their indeterminacy . . . But the silence imposed on knowledge does not impose the silence of forgetting, it imposes a feeling . . . The silence that surrounds the phrase, *Auschwitz was the extermination camp* is not a state of mind, it is the sign that something remains to be phrased which is not, something which is not determined.
>
> (1988a: 56–7)

Whole families and communities were systematically exterminated along with any evidence of their existences, and so even precise figures for the numbers of deaths (if such figures were available) can still not recover the names and identities of many who disappeared.

Beyond any evidence or statistics that can be adduced about the Holocaust, there is a feeling attached to it – the feeling arising from the wrong. According to Lyotard, if one pays attention to the differend of Auschwitz, this feeling becomes a 'sign' which explodes the empirical historical account by transforming Auschwitz from being just one more event in the continuity of history into something that calls the thinker to 'venture forth by lending his or her ear to what is not presentable under the rules of knowledge' (1988a: 57): to, in other words, explore the consequences for contemporary politics and culture of the occurrence of this differend. In Lyotard's reading, then, the differend of Auschwitz becomes a spur for thought, an ethical obligation addressed to the future that calls for analysis, discussion and justice. Beyond any statistical or empirical-historical accounting (both of which, however, are politically crucial), Auschwitz remains as a sign to be read by many of the contemporary genres of discourse, from literature and philosophy to anthropology and politics, each of which will find itself grasped by and reacting to the horror with its different resources for phrasing.

THE DIFFEREND, HISTORY AND THE DESTRUCTION OF GRAND NARRATIVES

The readings of Auschwitz in Lyotard's later works explore the effect it has as a horror that continues to cast its shadow over contemporary life. For Lyotard, it is not simply an event that has passed, after which history can continue on as normal. Instead, if one is to think historically in the aftermath of Auschwitz then that thinking must somehow be transformed. In an important essay from 1984, English translations of which have been reproduced in both *The Lyotard Reader* as 'Universal History and Cultural Differences' (1989: 314–23) and *The Postmodern Explained* as 'Missive on Universal History' (1992: 23–37), Lyotard describes the effects of Auschwitz on the idea of history.

Our sense of history, the way we organise and explain our past, is central to an individual's or a community's experience of itself and others, and also to its politics. History narrates the story of how we became who we are; it locates the present as part of a continuity and begins to point towards possible futures. As such, it is presented according to the rules of the narrative genre and, like literary narrative, can take a number of different forms. At the beginning of 'Universal History and Cultural Differences', Lyotard describes some of these forms, and links them to the major political and philosophical movements of modernity:

> The thought and action of the nineteenth and twentieth centuries are governed by an Idea (I am using Idea in its Kantian sense). That idea is the idea of emancipation. What we call philosophies of history, the great narratives by means of which we attempt to order the multitude of events, certainly argue this idea in very different ways . . . But they all situate the data supplied by events within the course of a history whose end, even if it is out of reach, is called freedom.
>
> (1989: 315)

Modern philosophies of history are tied to political systems and beliefs, each working towards its own notion of freedom. Examples Lyotard gives in the essay include Christianity, in which the sins of Adam and Eve will be redeemed by love and faith that will issue in a new Heaven on Earth, the Enlightenment narrative of the overcoming of superstition through knowledge and science which will lead to the freedom of a society that has been liberated from mysticism, the Marxist narrative of freedom from exploitation through the overthrow of injustices and class-divisions in the world, and Capitalism's narrative about the progress away from poverty through technical and industrial innovation and the free circulation of wealth to those who work.

In *The Postmodern Condition*, Lyotard describes these processes of organising history in terms of the idea of a progression towards freedom as grand narratives (see Chapter 1). These grand narratives are the organising principle for modernity, which, as Lyotard emphasises, 'is not an era in thought, but rather a mode . . . of thought, of utterance, of sensibility' (1989: 314), and can be described by means of the ideas of speculative and emancipatory grand narratives that he outlines there. However, as he claims in *The Postmodern Condition*, in postmodernity these grand narratives have lost their efficacy, and can no longer support a sense of universality. This means that the senses of history contained in them have to be rethought in the postmodern, and this is what the essay, 'Universal History and Cultural Differences', seeks to do. For this reason, Lyotard opens this essay with the question, 'can we continue today to organise the multitude of events that come to us from the world . . . by subsuming them beneath the idea of a universal history of humanity?' (1989: 314) This is a vital question for any attempt to discuss the relations between, for example, politics and culture or literature and philosophy, as each of these discourses will always be historically located and will, to at least some extent, be generated by the historical narrative from which it emerges. His answer to the question, however, is that we can't continue to organise experience around the idea of universal history: universal history, and the ideas of humanity, knowledge and emancipation that accompany it, are no longer possible.

'Universal History and Cultural Differences' gives a number of reasons why the world can no longer continue to be organised around such a sense of history. It lists some of the grand narratives, and cites events in the twentieth century that have thrown them into disorder:

> the very basis of each of the great narratives of emancipation has, so to speak, been invalidated over the last fifty years. All that is real is rational, all that is rational is real: 'Auschwitz' refutes speculative doctrine. At least that crime, which was real, was not rational. All that is proletarian is communist, all that is communist is proletarian: 'Berlin 1953, Budapest 1956, Czechoslovakia 1968, Poland 1980' (to mention only the most obvious examples) refute the doctrine of historical materialism: the

workers rise up against the Party. All that is democratic exists through and for the people, and vice versa: 'May 1968' refutes the doctrine of parliamentary liberalism. If left to themselves, the laws of supply and demand will result in universal prosperity, and vice versa: 'the crises of 1911 and 1929' refute the doctrine of economic liberalism.

(1989: 318)

Lyotard presents here a number of events that have become 'signs of history' due to the way they disrupt the rationales upon which some of the grand narratives are founded. In the first example he gives, Hegel's argument about speculative philosophy that logical thought can grasp reality, explain it and make use of it in the name of progress ('All that is real is rational'), meets its apotheosis in Auschwitz and the other death camps that make up this sign of history because nothing rational or progressive can be drawn from what happened there. Similarly, the Communist idea that the revolutionary parties work for and in the name of the working classes is challenged by a number of uprisings against the party such as, for example, the workers in the Polish shipyards at Gdansk who went on strike to protest against the Communist government in 1980 and formed the party, Solidarity, that was later to become a new government for Poland. In May 1968, students and workers throughout Europe and the United States protested against the violence of liberal parliamentary democracies and the wars that were being undertaken in their name despite their disapproval. Finally, the worldwide economic depression of 1929, Lyotard argues, refutes the capitalist idea that the free movement of money and goods leads necessarily towards the increase of wealth and freedom for all. Each of these examples strikes at the heart of one of the key organising principles of a grand narrative, challenging the system by which it shapes its construction of a historical progress towards an ideal of freedom.

These events thereby become 'so many signs of the defaillancy [the weakness, shortcoming or failure] of modernity' (1989: 318). The founding principles of modernity's grand narratives are challenged by events they should be able to explain, and collapse pointing the way towards the possibilities of postmodernity. The question Lyotard raises in the essay is how to follow on from these shortcomings in the grand narratives of modernity. He argues that there are several possibilities, and 'we have to decide between them. Even if we decide nothing, we still decide. Even if we remain silent, we speak . . . This is why the word *postmodernity* can refer simultaneously to the most disparate prospects' (1989: 319). In other words, the disruption of the grand narratives by events that remain inassimilable to them forces a reconsideration of the function and structure of historical enquiry. However, it is not the case that there is just one alternative: postmodern historiography can (and does) take a number of different forms according to the philosophical and political ideas and ends of the historian. Alternatively, and this is often what happens, one can continue to hold to the grand narrative despite the challenges issued to it under the 'signs of history'. Before moving on to describe Lyotard's account of the politics of history and the differend, I want briefly to outline two of the other key postmodern analyses of history that will serve as a helpful contrast to Lyotard.

HISTORY AND THE POSTMODERN: BAUDRILLARD AND JAMESON

Two recent theorists of the postmodern – Fredric Jameson and Jean Baudrillard – both take on board the transformation of historical enquiry in the second half of the twentieth century, and argue for the importance of thinking about history in relation to postmodernism. However, they do so from very different perspectives and with different aims. Jameson calls for a return to a Marxist analysis of history, and Baudrillard declares that history has been annihilated in the hyper-reality of contemporary media simulations.

Jameson, as a Marxist critic, argues that knowledge of history is extremely important for any discussion of culture and politics. In fact, he makes a case for the necessity of retaining the idea of history as a (Marxist) grand narrative if one is to produce a critical account of the present that can remain politically charged. Accordingly, historical events

> can recover their urgency for us only if they are retold within the unity of a single great collective story ... [which is] Marxism, the collective struggle to wrest a realm of Freedom from a realm of Necessity; only if they are grasped as vital episodes in a single vast unfinished plot.
>
> (Jameson 1981: 19–20)

In other words, for Jameson, the Marxist grand narrative is vital if one is to discuss culture and history in such a way as to keep in mind the importance of working towards human freedom.

In his influential book, *Postmodernism* (1991), Jameson describes postmodern culture as a turn away from historical thought that revels in an idea of history as nostalgia and something that can be reused by fashion: 'Nostalgia films restructure the whole issue . . . and project it onto a collective and social level, where the desperate attempt to appropriate a missing past is now refracted through the iron law of fashion change' (Jameson 1991: 19). For the postmodernist, Jameson argues, history becomes a matter of fashion. No longer thought of as the basis for a culture or a politics, history has become a matter for fashionable reappropriation in the media and arts where it loses its explanatory power. So, for example, the film *Forrest Gump* (1994) presents a sugar-coated view of American history to make (American) audiences feel good about who they are and to iron out any contradictions and difficulties present in US society and politics by presenting a pastiche of twentieth-century American life. The film has little radical political potential and serves only to reassure the audience that the American way, despite the problems it has faced during the last fifty years, is really the only way, and that everything will work out for the best if that way is followed.

For Jameson, this is one of the central problems of postmodernism. History has ceased in the culture of contemporary capitalism to be anything other than a commodity to be bought and sold as a 'stylistic connotation, conveying "pastness" by the glossy qualities of the image' (Jameson 1991: 19). Thus, the thrust of his work is to critique postmodernism's loss of history and urge the return to a Marxist version of the grand narrative.

Jean Baudrillard's work moves in a very different direction from Jameson's. Like Jameson he sees the postmodern as disrupting the possibility of thinking history as any form of grand narrative, and yet his writing presents postmodernism as a positive challenge to the 'sense-making' structure of any universal history. In *The Illusion of the End*, he argues that 'in the 1980s, history took a turn in the opposite direction' (Baudrillard 1994: 10). History, once thought of as a description of progress towards knowledge and freedom (what Lyotard identifies as a grand narrative), has turned in on itself as the time between the occurrence of events and their depiction in the media has become instantaneous, and the unifying thrust history was once supposed to have is transformed into an infinite multiplicity of competing interpretations whose sole purpose is to fill airtime. In the postmodern media age, Baudrillard argues,

> We may say of new events that they hollow out before them the void into which they plunge. They are intent, it seems, on one thing alone – being forgotten. They leave hardly any scope for interpretation, except for all interpretations at once, by which they evade any desire to give them meaning and elude the heavy attraction of a continuous history . . . They arrive – mostly unforeseen – more quickly than their shadows, but they have no sequel . . . One has the impression that events form all on their own and drift unpredictably towards their vanishing point – the peripheral void of the media.
>
> (1994: 19)

The media makes events instantaneously consumable and instantly forgettable as one moves inexorably onwards towards new information or further interpretation. With events seeming to move faster than the speed of light ('more quickly than their shadows'), a sense of cause and effect gets lost in the infinite multiplication of links and arguments as the media feeds frenziedly on 'angles' and commentaries. In this explosion of discussion, where the best interpretation seems to be nothing more than the one that works most quickly, the reality of the event itself disappears and the audience is left only with continually replayed and reworked simulations. This is the basis of Baudrillard's famously controversial argument that 'the Gulf War did not take place': because of the saturation of media coverage, the spectacular use of images that seemed to show no violence, the infinitely proliferating theories propounded by the pundits and commentators (including those representatives of the armaments industry who were keen to advertise the efficiency of their new weapons), and the fact that even the American army was forced to rely to a certain extent on the news channel CNN to find out the affects of its actions, Baudrillard claims it was impossible to separate simulation and propaganda from reality, even for those directly involved (see Baudrillard 1995).

THE DIFFEREND AND THE SIGN OF HISTORY

In contrast to these theorists Lyotard insists upon the importance of continuing to think and write history in the face of the disruption of the grand narratives. Unlike Jameson, he does not propose a return to a particular organising narrative. However, in distinction from Baudrillard, he does not argue a case for the complete disintegration of history. As the argument about the differend of Auschwitz presented in the first section of this chapter attempted to show, the task of the postmodern critic is not to condemn or celebrate some new age following on from the grand narratives of modernity, but to return continually to these events that have shaped contemporary genres of discourse in order to discover in them the voices that have been silenced.

In order to continue to discuss history in the wake of the collapse of the grand narratives, Lyotard again returns to Immanuel Kant's philosophy. Here he finds an account of history that continues to conceive of it as a whole rather than just a random series of unrelated events and yet refuses to produce the coercive account of historical progress (act according to this set of beliefs and the world will improve) that are the stuff of the grand narratives. This, therefore, places Lyotard's account of history somewhere between Baudrillard's media-based hyper-reality and Jameson's return to grand narrative legitimation. What allows this conception of history as a whole without making it into a grand narrative is Kant's distinction between concepts, which relate to specific things, and ideas that play a regulative role but are not open to direct experience (see Chapter 2, pp. 40–1). For Kant, 'history' and 'progress' are both ideas that produce the scheme in which specific events can be located, whereas each particular historical event is grasped and depicted by concepts. The aim of Kant's discussion of history is to raise the questions of how it is possible to be sure that history and progress exist, and, if they do, how they serve to organise the relations between particular events.

Kant argues that without an idea of the progress of history, 'men's actions on the great world-stage' would only appear to be 'an aimless course of nature, and blind chance', and concludes that the connection between history, moments and events must be underpinned by the 'guiding thread of reason' (Kant 1963: 12–13). In other words, if we can't discuss the connections between different events in history, all we are left with is a seemingly random patchwork of memories and simulations from the past.

When Kant attempts to describe this 'guiding thread' in 'An Old Question Raised Again: Is the Human Race Constantly Progressing?', he argues that 'the important thing is not the natural history of man . . . but rather his moral history and, more precisely, his history . . . as the totality of men united socially on earth and apportioned into peoples' (Kant 1963: 137). In other words, history for Kant is tied up with the ethical struggle to make the world fairer and more just. Like the grand narratives, Kant's view of history is about the progress of reason and freedom even if it doesn't result in the total-ising drive of such a grand narrative. What is required, therefore, is a demonstration that there is a 'disposition and capacity of the human race to be the cause of its own advance towards the better' (1963: 142). According to Kant, this demonstration must take the form of an 'event' that works as a 'historical sign that there is progress' (1963: 143).

Kant locates an event that acts as a 'sign of history' in the French Revolution, which took place at the end of the eighteenth century at the time when he was developing his philosophy. What he says is important about this event is not the Revolution itself, but the perspective taken towards it by observers in other countries:

> The revolution of a gifted people which we have seen unfolding in our day may succeed or miscarry; it may be filled with misery and atrocities to the point that a sensible man, were he boldly to hope to execute it successfully the second time, would never resolve to make the experi-ment at such cost – this revolution, I say, nonetheless finds in the hearts of all spectators (who are not engaged in this game themselves) a wishful participation that borders closely on enthusiasm, the very expression of which is fraught with danger; this sympathy, therefore, can have no other cause than a moral predisposition in the human race.
>
> (Kant 1963: 144)

What acts as a sign of the necessity of progress in this event is not the revolutionary action itself but the sympathy that it generates in those who are not directly involved. The fact that people who it does not directly involve support it and wish for its success, even if it puts them in danger in their own countries, demonstrates its moral importance. For Kant, what this enthusiasm indicates is nothing less than the 'moral predisposition' of humanity. In other words, for the onlookers, the French Revolution becomes a sign that there is moral progress towards the better. It doesn't tell them what they must do (those decisions are left open to them), but it does call for action in the face of those events.

What is crucial for Lyotard about Kant's account is that history is thought as a totality, but not presented as a grand narrative. All that can be concluded is that 'there is progress'. Lyotard explains this in the following way:

> This idea of necessity, which is the humblest one possible, excludes the capitalisation of history, for example, under the form of a totalising dialectic and thus excludes the 'semantic richness' that Jameson seems to expect from historicisation.

> (Lyotard 1984: 74)

Thus, Kant's deduction of progress refuses to set up a model for historical development from which an 'end of history' can be deduced and throws into question any single perspective or methodology for dealing with historical occurrences. All one is left with is the recognition that there is progress, that something must happen and be responded to. This is not Jameson's grand narrative, and yet it is significantly more substantial than Baudrillard's notion of the destruction of historical reference in the hyper-reality of media simulation.

Like Kant's account of the French Revolution, Lyotard's signs of history call for responses from the observers without predetermining what form those responses should take. Among these signs are the names and dates from 'Universal History and Cultural Differences' that were cited earlier in the chapter. Although they share a similar structure to Kant's sign, Lyotard's are less about progress and humanity's 'moral predisposition' than they are signs of a collapse of organising frameworks that present themselves as universal. In fact, each sign becomes for Lyotard a point at which conceptual and rational ways of organising history are called into question and new ways of thinking (new genres of discourse) have the potential to emerge.

Like the differend of Auschwitz discussed in the opening section, history as a collection of statistical data and empirical evidence is no longer able to deal adequately with the historical sign. Rather, the signs call for testimony and judgement from a range of genres (from literature, politics, philosophy, or even hitherto unrecognised modes of phrasing) to respond to the feelings that they bequeath:

> Each one of these abysses, and others, asks to be explored with precision in its specificity. The fact remains that all of them liberate judgement, that if they are to be felt, judgement must take place without a criterion, and that this feeling becomes in turn a sign of history. But however negative the signs to which most of the proper names of our political history give rise, we should nevertheless have to judge them *as if* they proved that this history had moved on a step in its progress . . . This step would consist in the fact that it is not only the Idea of a *single* purpose which would be pointed to in our feeling, but already the Idea that this purpose consists in the formation and free exploration of Ideas *in the plural*, the idea that this end is the beginning of the *infinity of heterogeneous finalities*.

> (1989: 409)

What Lyotard is getting at here is that the judgements called for by what he has identified as signs of history point not to a new grand narrative, but rather to a fracturing of history into an infinite plurality of narratives and genres, each of which allows different voices and possibilities to emerge. The sign of history is thus an 'abyss' for knowledge: it explodes the genres of discourse that seek to contain and explain it, and remains for posterity as a 'feeling' that calls for a 'judgement without criterion'. The event itself that is the basis of the sign is unpresentable, but the sign presents the fact of its existence – it is sublime. The task of the historical thinker is thus to attempt to read these signs much in the manner that one might attempt to read a postmodern work of literature or art. There are no rules for these readings that explain meanings in advance, and no reading is ever final or determinate. Instead, readings must always be open and plural, acknowledging the sign's uniqueness and singularity. The guiding thread is always Lyotard's ethical notion of opening up genres of discourse to find new ways to phrase what is excluded from them.

SUMMARY

Lyotard argues that postmodernity marks the point where universalising accounts of history break down. He claims that there are certain events whose impacts on particular ideas of universal progress make them into signs of the disruption of modernity's grand narratives. In *The Differend*, the key instance of this is Auschwitz, the Nazi concentration camp. Here, Lyotard argues, the speculative grand narrative founders in the face of absolute barbarity. This and other signs are open to more than just statistical or empirical description, however. Instead, they call for responses from across the range of possible genres of discourse.

In contrast to other postmodernist writers, such as Fredric Jameson who urges a return to a Marxist version of history or Jean Baudrillard whose work stages the annihilation of the historical referent by modern communications, Lyotard insists on the importance of paying attention to the signs of history. Following Kant, he argues that history must be thought of as an idea but that contemporary signs of history point to the irreducible plurality of historical schemes, and that it is this plurality that provides the focus for criticism.

5

ART, THE INHUMAN
AND THE EVENT

Chapter 2 began to explore the arguments for art's importance that are set out in 'An Answer to the Question: What is the Postmodern?'. There Lyotard deployed the Kantian concept of the sublime as the key means by which art is capable of presenting the fact that something always remains unpresentable: that any language game (or genre of discourse to use the category introduced in *The Differend*) excludes certain possibilities of speaking, silences particular voices and fails to represent the importance of some events. Postmodern art was described as a means by which this silencing exclusion could be indicated and exposed. Through formal experimentation, postmodern art and literature can present the fact of the unpresentable's existence and force the recognition that art can be disorientating, that it has the potential actively to question received ideas about reality and challenge the genres of discourse that emerge with them.

The previous two chapters, at least to a certain extent, left art in the background while discussing the importance of the sublime for Lyotard's analyses of ethics, politics and history. However, because of the relation between the sublime, the differend and the sign of

hould be clear that issues relating to art and aesthetics
ar from the surface of his thinking. The differend and the
give rise to sublime feelings, and the ethical obligation
of testifying to them is, for Lyotard, a task that art is particularly
well equipped to perform. Because of this it is often employed as a
model in his analyses of what testimony entails. Art is thus both
a model for thinking the differend, and also a key site where the
consensus generated by a genre of discourse can be challenged. The
aim of this chapter is to begin to introduce some of Lyotard's analyses
of how these challenges emerge, and to demonstrate the important
roles that art and literature play in his postmodern philosophy.

THE ROLE OF ART

Throughout his work, Lyotard was a champion of the creative artist,
and it is worth recapping briefly on the place that art holds in some
of the texts that this book has examined so far before turning to his
work on particular artists and writers. It is important to remember
here that Lyotard's account of postmodern art does not posit it as
simply the latest thing in artistic or narrative style. He is not interested in questions of fashion or playfulness. Rather, the role of art is
to disturb or disrupt consensus and to make possible the emergence
of new forms and voices that increase the range of possible ways to
phrase experience.

In 'An Answer to the Question: What is the Postmodern?', he
compares the postmodern artist to a philosopher, arguing that

> The postmodern artist or writer is in the position of a philosopher: the
> text he writes or the work he creates is not in principle governed by
> pre-established rules . . . Such rules and categories are what the work
> or text is investigating. The artist and the writer therefore work without
> rules and in order to establish the rules for *what will have been made*.
> This is why the work and the text can take on the properties of an event.
>
> (1992: 15)

What Lyotard means by this should perhaps be clearer after having examined his arguments in *The Differend*. The postmodern work of art is not one that develops according to the rules of a pre-established genre of discourse. Rather, in attempting to present that there is an unpresentable, it searches for new means of expression and new rules for presentation. It occurs as an event that disrupts and challenges what hitherto had been thought of as the rules of artistic presentation, and thereby has the potential to generate new genres of discourse and new openings for knowledge and politics. This notion of the 'event' is crucial to Lyotard's aesthetics, and will become the focus of discussion later in this chapter.

Lyotard's arguments in *The Differend* expand upon the ideas in 'An Answer to the Question' to set out the crucial place that literature occupies in relation to thought and politics: 'What is at stake in a literature, in a philosophy, in a politics perhaps, is to bear witness to differends by finding idioms for them' (1988a: 13). The differend, the site of a conflict where one or more of the opposing parties is condemned to silence, calls for testimony. It is not a question of resolving a differend according some set of pre-established rules. Instead, the existence of the conflict that engenders it must be brought to light and new means of bearing witness must be sought. Art's and literature's ability and freedom to experiment with ideas and forms, to experimentally rewrite the rules of discourse, make it a crucial tool for seeking these means. Placed alongside politics and philosophy (and art is always discussed in terms of this relation by Lyotard), literature is a key means of questioning dominant genres and exposing the differends they suppress.

These statements point towards the idea that art and literature are related to the potential for transformation. Art, according to Lyotard, does not simply reflect reality. Rather it intervenes in the genres of discourse that construct a given reality and opens up possibilities for disruption and change. In all of his discussions of aesthetics, it is art's potential to challenge established ideas and systems that remains the point of focus.

This potential is described most clearly in the introduction to Lyotard's important book from 1988, *The Inhuman: Reflections on Time*. Here, he argues that contemporary culture imposes an injunction on art, as well as on thought generally, which is the prescription of realism: 'Be communicable, that is the prescription. Avant-garde is old hat, talk about humans in a human way, address yourself to human beings, if they enjoy receiving you then they will receive you' (1991a: 2). This is the same attack on experimentation that Lyotard challenged in 'An Answer to the Question'. According to this formulation, avant-garde art and literature is presented as inaccessible, anti-human and unenjoyable, and instead, the artist or writer is called upon to appeal to the human and her or his potential for enjoyment. In the contemporary marketplace, the value of art is presented as its ability to appeal to a mass audience, and the best way to ensure success is to communicate quickly and pleasantly, and in an immediately accessible manner. However, Lyotard is suspicious of this notion of art's task as talking about 'humans in a human way' and strongly resists the idea that art is just another mere commodity. As his discussions of language games and phrases make clear, what a particular culture thinks of as 'the human' is only ever the accepted construct of whichever genres of discourse happen to be the organising principles for that social group. In the contemporary drive for technological efficiency and the tendency to reduce all questions to those of saving money or time, which was identified with capitalism in *The Postmodern Condition*, Lyotard argues that the 'human' is reduced to a technical product: the sum of its genes, the result of its upbringing, the product of its labour, etc. In this way, he claims, the human is being transformed into something inhuman by the capitalist 'vanguard machine' that drags 'humanity after it, dehumanising it' in the drive for ultimate efficiency (1984: 63). Being explained, the human ceases to have the capacity to be surprising or strange and is reduced to just another cog in the machine of capitalism (or Marxism, or Christianity, to mention just two more grand narratives).

In contrast to this technological inhuman, Lyotard claims that art points towards another form of the inhuman: the potential for being taken hold of by surprising and uncanny transformative possibilities that cannot be predicted, explained or mastered by technologically-based systems of reason. He locates this sense of the inhuman in the 'anguish of a mind haunted by a familiar and unknown guest which is agitating it, sending it delirious but also making it think' (1991a: 2). This inhuman is another version of those figures that Lyotard has employed to indicate the postmodern: it works in the same sort of way as the sublime, the differend and the sign to open up the possibility of thinking events without pre-given structures of thought. It is at once disturbing and potentially liberating, and the task of thought is to bear witness to it.

The figure that Lyotard associates with this second form of inhumanity in *The Inhuman* is the child. He argues that the fact that 'children have to be educated is a circumstance which only proceeds from the fact that they are not completely led by nature, not programmed' (1991a: 3). The child, as a bundle of unsocialised wants and desires points to something within the human that is not determined wholly by the dominant genres that surround its 'development'. It is not that a child is 'more human' than the adult as some of the educational ideas of the nineteenth century might argue, but rather that its 'unprogrammed' state at the moment of its entry into the world points to a potential site for resistance to domination by social organisation that remains within each and every adult.

For Lyotard, then, the human is the product of a conflict between two inhumans: the inhuman systems of capitalist development and technology threaten to extinguish anything in the human that is not of value to them, and yet within this same human lies the uncanny strangeness of another inhuman that is a potential site of resistance. He argues that,

> the question I am raising here is simply this: what else remains as 'politics' except resistance to this inhuman [system]? And what else is left

to resist with but the debt to which each soul has contracted with the miserable and admirable indetermination from which it was born and does not cease to be born? – which is to say, with the other inhuman?

This debt to childhood is one which we never pay off . . . It is the task of writing, thinking, literature, arts, to venture to bear witness to it.

(1991a: 7)

Without the inhuman indetermination at its heart – the debt to the unsocialised child – the human ceases to be able to resist the other form of the inhuman, that of the developmental system. As Lyotard argues in a later essay, 'The right to this no-man's-land is the very foundation of human rights . . . Humanity is only human if people have this "no-man's-land"' (1997: 116). As the closing sentence in the long quotation above states, art's and literature's 'task' is to bear witness to the 'no-man's-land' and militate against the drive to exclude it from the systems and genres that seek to explain entirely and control it. It is thus that art stages a defence of humanity.

Perhaps the most powerful example of the role and importance of the second sense of the inhuman in artistic testimony appears in two texts that Lyotard published before *The Postmodern Condition*: *Libidinal Economy* (1974) and *Duchamp's TRANS/formers* (1977).

MARCEL DUCHAMP AND THE INDUSTRIAL INHUMAN

The text that sealed Lyotard's break with his old Marxist colleagues from the group *Socialisme ou Barbarie* was *Libidinal Economy*. Here, Lyotard attacks Marxism head-on, splitting the figure of Karl Marx into two characters, each of whom represents a different relation to capitalism found in Marx's texts: the first is 'Old Man Marx' who scientifically describes the ills of capitalism and provides sets of laws to determine its overthrow, and the second is 'Little Girl Marx' who is seduced by it and enters into a love affair with capitalism's perverse body (1993a: 97). In this way, Lyotard argues that Marxism exists in a paradoxical relationship with capitalism as it simultaneously condemns it and is captivated by it. This split anticipates his discussions of the inhuman: the Old Man Marx is the systematiser, the producer of Marxism's grand narrative that presses everything into its mould, whereas the Little Girl points towards the sense of the inhuman as exceeding reason by constantly haunting the system with desire and seduction.

Lyotard's conversion of Marx into a 'strange bisexual assemblage' (1993a: 96) is not simply done to offend his ex-colleagues (though it certainly achieved this). Rather, it highlights the ways in which capitalism 'exceeds the capacity of theoretical discourse' (Marxism) to explain its effects (1993a: 98). Due to its love–hate relationship with capitalism, he argues, Marxism's analyses remain complicit with the latter's conception of social change as a grand narrative of development, and in the end both are only able to depict the people caught up in capitalism as objects of this development. Both Marxism and capitalism produce systems to explain development that leave no room for the possibility of the second sense of inhumanity within those caught up in it. Lyotard argues that their descriptions of the rise of modern capitalism during the Industrial Revolution of the nineteenth century depict the working classes as little more than cattle who were dragged backwards through the changes that took place (1990b: 16–17). In contrast to this, in a passage that particularly scandalised his critics, he draws the following alternative picture of industrialisation:

> look at the English proletariat, at what capital, that is to say *their labour*, has done to their body. You will tell me, however, that it was that [i.e. go to work for the capitalists] or die . . . And perhaps you believe that 'that or die' is an *alternative*?! And that if they choose that, if they become the slave of the machine, the machine of the machine, fucker fucked by it, eight hours, twelve hours, a day, year after year, it was because they were forced into it, constrained, because they cling to life? Death is not an alternative to it, it is part of it, it attests to the fact that there

is *jouissance* in it, the English unemployed did not become workers to
survive, they – hang on tight and spit on me – *enjoyed* the hysterical,
masochistic, whatever exhaustion it was of *hanging on* in the mines, the
foundries, in the factories, in hell, they enjoyed it, enjoyed the mad
destruction of their organic body which was indeed imposed upon them,
they enjoyed the decomposition of their personal identity, the identity
the peasant tradition had constructed for them, enjoyed the dissolution
of their families and villages, and enjoyed the new monstrous *anonymity*
of the suburbs and the pubs in the morning and evening.

(Lyotard 1993a: 111)

This is a highly controversial argument, and one that brought a great
deal of criticism down on Lyotard's head. In effect, what he is saying
is that there is in the working-class experience of industrialisation the
possibility of 'enjoyment' or '*jouissance*'. He implies that the workers
entered into some sort of bizarre masochistic relation with capitalism, and that they consented to the pain and suffering that
their bodies underwent in the mines and factories. However, it is
important to note that Lyotard is certainly not arguing that capitalist
exploitation and the suffering it produces are good things. The key
term here is '*jouissance*'. The English term, 'enjoyment', that is used
to translate it does not convey the full force of meaning that is
contained in the French. *Jouissance* means pleasure, but suggests also
ecstasy and sexual orgasm. It immediately points to what is beyond
the bounds of rational thought, excessive with regard to conscious
control, and also suggests the possibility of transformation (through
conception and birth). Lyotard plays on all of these senses to argue
that what happens to the workers in the factories is nothing less than
a transformation of their humanity. Working in this 'hell' they
change: their bodies alter to cope with the conditions and their experiences of their relations to the world are converted from those of
rural agriculture to the suburbs of the new cities. In *Libidinal Economy*
it is thus the bodies and desires of the workers themselves that
contain the possibility of transformation and become the site for

critical engagement. More precisely, change emerges from the inhuman *jouissance* within their identities that allows them to survive the inhumanity of the factories and mines.

According to Lyotard in *Duchamp's TRANS/formers*, this transformation of the human body is captured in the work of the French avant-garde artist, Marcel Duchamp (1887–1968). Duchamp's art feeds upon the detritus of industrialism. He is famous for his 'ready-mades', found objects such as a bicycle wheel or a urinal that are transformed into art simply by being placed in a gallery and given a title, as well as his pieces that distort the human body such as 'Nude Descending a Staircase' (1913) which depicts through a series of strokes the movement of a body as it descends from left to right across the canvas, 'The Bride Stripped Bare by her Bachelors, even (The Large Glass)' (1912) that places a collection of mechanical objects in a glass case to allude to a scene of undressing observed by a group of men, or 'Given 1. The Waterfall, 2. The Illuminating Gas' (1946–66) in which a naked female torso lying near a waterfall is seen through a slot in a door.

Lyotard reads Duchamp's art as pointing towards a similar *jouissance* to that played out on the workers' bodies. It is not that Duchamp depicts the factories (he doesn't) or that the works are about history (they aren't). Rather, Lyotard points to the way in which his paintings and sculptures disorientate the spectator by taking a human figure or an everyday object and transforming it into something strange, disturbing or even funny – something that is, precisely, inhuman. There is thus an analogy between what happened to the workers and what is presented in Duchamp's art. Both, he argues, lead to 'the demeasurement of what was held to be the human, to the toleration of situations that were thought to be intolerable' (Lyotard 1990b: 15). In the sphere of art, Duchamp's avant-garde challenge to established beliefs about what a work of art should be undermines the sense of the stability of the human figure just as the experience of the workers disrupted ideas about what human beings could survive. In the light of Duchamp's art and under the shadow of industrialisation, the sense of what it is to be human alters. For Lyotard, though, Duchamp does not present an alternative account of the human. Rather, his art testifies to the inhuman at its centre: through the disturbingly humorous ways in which it disrupts the human body and its surroundings, Duchamp's art refuses to be tied down or explained as it provokes us to respond to it.

NINETEEN EIGHTY-FOUR AND THE RESISTANCE TO TOTALITARIANISM

Duchamp's work is thus presented by Lyotard as a site where the second sense of the inhuman appears to testify to the annihilation of prior categories of the human by industrial development. This approach to art and literature as a site where disruption is figured or presented continues throughout his work on the postmodern. For an example of this from literature it is worth turning to a later essay called 'A Gloss on Resistance' collected in *The Postmodern Explained*, in which Lyotard discusses *Nineteen Eighty-Four* by the English novelist and essayist, George Orwell (1903–50). Here, Lyotard makes a case for the importance of thinking the clash between the inhuman system, the possibility of resistance within it, and the scope of literature as a means of bringing this resistance into focus.

Orwell's *Nineteen Eighty-Four* tells the story of Winston Smith, a citizen of 'Airstrip One' (which is a futuristic Britain that has become an outpost of an American Empire called 'Oceania') in which everything is regulated by the government of a sinister 'Big Brother'. People's lives are tightly controlled and they are constantly observed by 'telescreens' that also pour out propaganda. Language is becoming more and more restricted as 'Newspeak' is developed and old English words discarded. Even the citizens' innermost beliefs are subject to investigation by the 'Thought Police'. The novel traces Winston's resistance to the authority of the government, and his eventual capture and interrogation. He keeps an illegal secret diary, enters into an unauthorised affair with a young co-worker called

Julia, and is eventually tricked by the party official, O'Brien, into pledging allegiance to a (possibly imaginary) terrorist group that leads to his arrest by the Thought Police.

From this synopsis of the plot, it might seem that *Nineteen Eighty-Four* is a fairly hopeless place to look for revolutionary activity as Winston's defiance of the state is ineffectual, and his defeat by O'Brien absolute. However, it is not the actions of the central character that interest Lyotard. Rather, his essay takes its point of departure from the way in which Orwell's novel challenges the totalitarian society it depicts by its own status as literature. Lyotard argues that, in *Nineteen Eighty-Four*,

> Orwell does not put forward a theoretical critique of bureaucracy. This novel of totalitarianism does not set out to be a political theory . . . But literary writing, artistic writing, because it demands privation, cannot cooperate with the project of domination or total transparency, even involuntarily.
>
> (1992: 88)

What Lyotard is suggesting here is that there is something within the very genre of literary writing which resists the forms of bureaucratic domination that ask for total transparency by reducing everything to their own explanatory genres of discourse. Criticism is itself a form of domination if it presents an overall explanation of a text, but that criticism is also doomed to failure as there is something in the text that 'cannot cooperate' with it. In other words, literature and art themselves are modes of resistance. The question is, what form does this resistance take?

Lyotard's discussion of *Nineteen Eighty-Four* opens by focusing on Winston's decision to keep the illegal diary, which he describes as 'an initial act of resistance' (1992: 88). The diary itself is a mixture of revolutionary statements, and the memories and feelings elicited by the act of writing. The writing is a form of discovery: through keeping the diary Winston recalls forgotten moments in his life as well as making connections between them and the present that hitherto had not been possible. For Lyotard, this writing is both resistance to totalitarianism and weakness in the face of it. The construction of a narrative in the diary reveals that the domination by Big Brother is not total as it elicits ideas that cannot finally be repressed by the bureaucratic order. At the same time, though, the writing is weak and produces a point of defencelessness in Winston: on being discovered, the diary is used by O'Brien to break Winston down during the interrogation. Lyotard argues that this combination of resistance and weakness occurs in every act of writing, and particularly literary writing: 'Writing must perform on itself – in its detail, in the restlessness of words as they appear or fail to appear, in its receptivity to the contingency of the word – the very work of exploring its own weakness and energy . . . in the face of the insidious threat of totalitarianism' (1992: 89).

This analysis of the writing of the diary allows Lyotard to open up a discussion about the resistance of writing itself. He argues that literary writing and artistic creation, work to oppose the closure of systems and serve as a means of exposing their potential for disruption. He claims that, 'One writes against language, but necessarily with it . . . One violates it, one seduces it, one introduces into it an idiom unknown to it' (1992: 89). Literary writing employs language, but introduces into that language new idioms (modes of speaking or, to use Lyotard's terms, ways of linking phrases). In this way, writing generates a space for the apprehension of what Lyotard calls the 'event'. In contrast to this, the system attempts to control events, to calculate their value and reduce their meaning to pre-established categories: in other words, the event 'goes into the dustbin (of history, of spirit). An event will be retrieved only if it illustrates the master's views' (1992: 90).

According to Lyotard then, the task of the artist or writer is to

fight against the cicatrisation of the event, against its categorisation as 'childishness', to preserve initiation. This is the fight fought by writing against bureaucratic Newspeak. Newspeak has to tarnish the wonder that (something) is happening.

(1992: 91)

In other words, the key power of art and literature is to bear witness to the occurrence of what he calls an 'event'. In contrast to systematic thought, which seeks to comprehend these events according to what is already understood about the world, art presents their occurrence without necessarily providing exhaustive analyses or explanations of them. It opens up the world to investigation and thought by allowing it to be surprising. The question that arises from this is thus, what does Lyotard mean by 'event'?

THE EVENT

The idea of 'event' is crucial to many of the themes in Lyotard's thought that this book has explored so far. An event challenges established genres of discourse and calls for all that has lead up to it to be rethought. In many ways it is the founding moment of any postmodernism. Bill Readings, one of the most incisive commentators on Lyotard's work, defines the event in the following manner:

An event is an occurrence, as such . . . That is to say, the event is the fact or case that something happens, after which nothing will ever be the same again. The event disrupts any pre-existing referential frame within which it might be represented or understood. The eventhood of the event is the radical *singularity* of happening, the 'it happens' as distinct from the sense of 'what is happening'.

(Readings 1991: xxxi)

This is a complex description, but one that goes to the heart of Lyotard's idea. The aim of this section is to begin to make clear what the implications of it are and how art and literature are exemplary locations for the occurrence of events in Lyotard's thought.

Some of Lyotard's most detailed discussions of the meaning of 'event', and its relationship to art occur in two essays on the avant-garde American artist, Barnett Newman (1905–1970), which are collected in *The Inhuman*: 'Newman: the Instant' and 'The Sublime and the Avant-Garde'. What draws Lyotard to Newman is the apparent simplicity of his work: his paintings often consist of little more than one or more vertical lines set onto washes of a single colour. This minimalism expresses for Lyotard a resistance to the social conditioning of capitalism and the humanist idea that art should represent the world or tell a story about it. He argues that a 'canvas by Newman draws a contrast between stories and its plastic nudity . . . What can one say that is not given? It is not difficult to describe, but the description is as flat as a paraphrase . . . There is almost nothing to "consume"' (1991a: 80). The response to a Newman painting is thus instantaneous. One is confronted by an image that needs no time to take in or interpret, which alludes to no hidden meanings, and seems to conceal no complex technique to be deciphered. And yet this image arrests the viewer, stopping them in their tracks and eliciting a sense of the sublime.

According to Lyotard, the sublime feeling generated by a Newman painting provides access to another sense of time, the time of the event, which disrupts the everyday consciousness of experience:

> Newman's *now* which is no more than *now* is a stranger to consciousness and cannot be constituted by it. Rather, it is what dismantles consciousness, what deposes consciousness, it is what consciousness cannot formulate, even what consciousness forgets in order to constitute itself. What we do not manage to formulate is that something happens . . . Or rather, and more simply, that it happens . . . Not a major event in the media sense, not even a small event. Just an occurrence . . . An event, an occurrence . . . is infinitely simple, but this simplicity can only be approached through a state of privation. That which we call thought must be disarmed.

> (1991a: 90)

Because there is so little to think about in a Newman painting and yet its impact on the viewer is so immediate and powerful, one's conscious critical powers are disarmed. The apparent simplicity of the painting evokes the sublime feeling that something has happened without the knowledge of what it is. It demands a reaction from the spectator without giving any clues about what the painting represents. One has the sense that something has happened, but it seems impossible to decide quite what that something is. The difference between 'something happens' and 'what happens' is crucial. To be able to say 'what happens' is already to have understood the meaning of an event, to have drawn it into consciousness and fitted it into a genre or genres of discourse. On the other hand, the 'something happens' calls for a receptivity to the event itself, a reaction to it that is not guided by pre-given guidelines and a questioning of those genres of discourse that appear unable adequately to fit it into their schemes of thought. In this form of response, the event resists representation (it is, in itself, unpresentable), and yet it challenges those established modes of representation as they attempt to suppress its strangeness. This distinction between the 'something' and the 'what' is the basis for Lyotard's philosophy of the event.

We might thus reformulate the last quotation to say that for Lyotard an event consists in the perception of an instant in which something happens to which we are called to respond without knowing in advance the genre in which to respond. In other words, events occur in such a way that pre-established genres are incapable of responding adequately to their singular nature. The event might be something as simple as a painting or a poem, or as complex and world changing as Auschwitz or the French Revolution. Throughout Lyotard's work, the event is what calls for a response, a judgement, which respects its specificity and refuses simply to fit it into a pre-given scheme.

In the case of Newman, and avant-garde art more generally, the eventhood of the works stages the refusal of art to be reduced to political propaganda or commodity. For Lyotard, it is the structure of capitalist speculation in which the 'experience of the human subject – individual and collective – and the aura that surrounds this experience, are being dissolved into the calculation of profitability' that art's relation to the event stands to unsettle (1991a: 105). If a work of art can hold within itself the minimal instance of an event, it retains something that is irreducible to systematic comprehension or exploitation. Judged from the perspective of its eventhood, a work of art has the potential to uncover differends submerged in the genres of discourse that shape social life. Criticism, for Lyotard, begins with the event, and its task is to work through the implications of the work of art's irreducibility to established ideas and practices.

SUMMARY

Works of art and literature, according to Lyotard, do not offer direct answers to political and philosophical problems. Rather, their value lies in an ability to generate questions that can challenge ways of thinking and genres of discourse that attempt to provide all-encompassing explanations and systems. In other words, the work of art or literature has the capacity to expose the differends that these genres conceal. Lyotard refers to this capacity as a form of the inhuman. In contrast to the inhumanity of the totalising or totalitarian system, art can evoke feelings of disturbance or disorientation that are irreducible to rational thought or calculation. These feelings, he argues, mark an inhuman 'no-man's-land' at the heart of the human subject that resists total explanation and appropriation by genres of discourse.

Because of its appeal to this childlike, unconditioned inhuman within the human and its capacity always to exceed theoretical description, Lyotard argues that the work of art appears as an event. This notion of the event is vital to Lyotard's thought. It marks the point at which something happens that has the potential to shatter prior ways of explaining and making sense of the world and calls for new modes of experience and different forms of judgement.

6

THE TASK OF THE CRITIC: REWRITING MODERNITY

The opening chapter of the 'Key Ideas' section focused on *The Postmodern Condition*, the book that introduced Lyotard's work most widely to the English-speaking world. The discussions in subsequent chapters have taken different areas of Lyotard's work on themes, issues and ideas related to the postmodern and explored them in more detail. The aim of this final chapter is to bring those different discussions back together in order to explore the implications of the postmodern in more detail as well as introduce ideas about the sort of critical responses that Lyotard might encourage us to have to contemporary culture and politics.

Each of the last four chapters ended by arguing that Lyotard's thought generates ways to destabilise and disrupt those systematic theories that attempt to provide totalising or universal explanations, whether they be theories of art and literature, politics, philosophy or history. The primary aim of Lyotard's writing is, through these disruptions, to allow different voices and new ways of thinking, writing and acting in the world to emerge. By presenting that there is an unpresentable, art and literature can transform established ways of writing or picturing the world and intervene in social, political and cultural debates. Through testifying to the existence of differends the critic can open up new possibilities for thought and action and allow those voices threatened with silence to be heard. Investigation of the signs of history can discover those points at which the grand narratives of modernity are called into question and ways are opened to more pluralist modes of thinking history and the present. In each of these cases, the occurrence of a sublime moment, differend or sign has the status of an event: impossible to predict, something happens that is irreducible to established critical or political criteria and calls for judgement.

There is little doubt that the conclusions Lyotard reaches across a range of discussions have profound implications for the ways in which we might think about contemporary life, and yet some readers might well be left with the nagging suspicion that something is missing. Lyotard uncovers the moments and modes in which genres of discourse are opened to disruption and challenges are issued to the legitimacy of modernity's grand narratives, and yet his writing offers little in terms of a programme for thought or action in response to them. Having discovered a differend, for example, what is one supposed to do with it?

Lyotard's apparent refusal to provide guidance for dealing with events or even to set out a system into which they can be inserted seems to have annoyed some of his commentators quite intensely. To cite just one example of this, in *Lyotard and the End of Grand Narratives* Gary Browning complains about the difficulty of a direct application of Lyotard's ideas to public politics:

> Lyotard emphasises that there is no meta-discourse into which *differends* can be translated, reworked and remedied. The upshot of this valorisation of a non-discursive sublime feeling is that difference is taken to constitute a universal limit, precluding the possibilities involved in individuals making and experiencing an inter-subjective world in which their different interests can be satisfied along with

The problem for Browning here is that Lyotard's focus on the disruption of metanarrative structures appears to preclude the possibility
of agreement between different groups or cultures as well as denying
the critic an ability to generate a public consensus about the ways
in which a society should be made fair. Like Fredric Jameson, he
concludes that 'Lyotard is too ready to dismiss the notion of self-
consciously developing a grand narrative' (2000: 171), and urges a
recognition of the importance of continuing the critical processes of
a Hegelian or Marxist notions of modernity. Browning's critique
(and the defence of modernity to which it leads) is not only levelled
at the differend through the genre of politics – it might apply equally
to most of Lyotard's arguments about the postmodern. Each of the
discussions in the preceding chapters has ended with a moment of
disruption, whether it is the sublime, the differend, the sign or the
event. But the questions that may well arise are, what comes next?
What does Lyotard tell us about how we should read a text, understand a work or, even, change the world? What is it we are supposed
to *do* with sublimity, signs, differends and events?

These are important and genuine questions. Crucially, however,
they are ones that Lyotard refuses to answer: he does not espouse a
particular philosophical methodology or a specific political doctrine
any more than he presents final or incontrovertible readings of pieces
of art or literature. In short, there is no 'Lyotardian system' that
provides in advance answers to the potential questions or problems
thrown up by works and events. In fact, from the foregoing discussions in this book it should be clear that there could not possibly be
such a system, because to erect one would be to betray his most
fundamental insights about differends, signs and events. Because each
of these figures is sublime, because it presents that there is an unpresentable that is irreducible to genres of thought or politics and calls

for something new, to develop a system that explains them and anticipates their appearance would immediately be to deny their
eventhood. In other words, such a system would, to adopt the question that ends *The Differend*, 'prejudge the *Is it happening?*' (see 1988a:
181). In other words, it would explain the meaning of an event
before its occurrence and thereby eliminate its transformative potential by fitting it into what is already known. To read Lyotard, one
must take into account this refusal to prejudge events and differends.
If one is to follow on from his thinking, what is required is openness
to what is surprising, and attentiveness to the possibilities that the
event's disruption of established genres might reveal. This is, at
the same time, both frustrating ('why doesn't he give us some
answers?') and exhilarating as it allows (or, rather, forces) us to think
for ourselves.

The question that this chapter will address, then, is what is the
role of the critic or thinker that is constructed in Lyotard's writing?
Or, in other words, what space does his work generate for others'
philosophical, political or critical analyses and discussions? The
chapter begins by outlining Lyotard's arguments about Kant's
distinction between determinate and reflective judgements, and his
valorisation of the latter as a tool for critical thinking. From here, it
will move on to examine his analyses about the importance of reflectively judging the culture of modernity, and finally will discuss his
last writings on the French writer and revolutionary André Malraux
(1901–76) to give an example of Lyotard's method of rewriting
modernity through readings of art and culture.

POSTMODERN THINKING: REFLECTIVE AND DETERMINATE JUDGEMENT

As is probably apparent by now, Kant's influence on Lyotard
is profound. More than he does with any other writer, Lyotard
returns continually to Kant in order to discover the tools for thinking
about our contemporary culture. We have already discussed the

importance for Lyotard of Kant's distinctions between concepts and ideas, epistemology and ethics, and his analyses of the sublime and the sign of history. However, there is one argument of Kant's that is, perhaps, even more fundamental for Lyotard's construction of a postmodern philosophy: the distinction between determinate and reflective judgement.

The notion of reflective judgement is developed by Kant in the *Critique of Judgement* in order to explain the way people respond to aesthetic experiences, but its ramifications are much wider than just thought about art. According to the third *Critique*,

> Judgement is the ability to think the particular as contained under the universal. If the universal (the rule, principle, law) is given, then judgement, which subsumes the particular under it, is *determinative* . . . But if only the particular is given and judgement has to find the universal for it, then this power is . . . *reflective*.
>
> (Kant 1987: 18–19)

The basis of judgement, according to this quotation, is the generation of a relation between particular perceptions or experiences and the universal concepts that allow the subject to identify them and say what they are. In other words, to recognise a particular piece of furniture as a chair, we need to be able to relate the sense impression of that object to the concept 'chair'. This concept is universal because it can be applied to all of the different chairs that one comes across, despite the particular differences between each one (whether it is red or brown, wood or plastic, hard or upholstered, we must still be able to bring it under the concept 'chair' in order to identify it). To put this in the language of *The Differend*, judgement is what decides upon which genre of discourse will be applicable to explain and understand a particular state of affairs.

The difference between a determinate and a reflective judgement emerges from the different means by which this relation between concepts and experiences comes about. A determinate judgement, which is really the sort we make most of the time, occurs when we fit a new experience into our existing conceptual structure. This means that determinate judgements tend to be processes of recognition. Or, in other words, one's recognition of something emerges from the ability to relate a particular experience of it to concepts that we already have: so, for example, we recognise a particular appearance of a small furry nut-eating animal with a long bushy tail because we already have a concept of what a squirrel is. Alternatively, we can tell the difference between a play-script and a novel because the literary critical genre of discourse has given us the conceptual tools to distinguish between the two. We tend to be able to do this without much thought – the squirrel and the play-script appear to us 'naturally' to be what they are.

In contrast to determinate judgements, reflective judgement takes place when something new, different or strange appears, and we struggle to come to terms with what it is or means. The particular experience takes place and we are forced desperately to search for a way of conceptualising it. This might occur in relation to a piece of modern art that baffles our expectations (in fact Kant and Lyotard both argue that this should happen in all aesthetic experience), or when we are confronted by the rituals of a culture with which we are unfamiliar. Our existing conceptual criteria seem not to apply to the specific case, so rather than employing them we judge reflectively and attempt to search for a rule that will make things make sense and guide our responses to them. With regard to Lyotard's categories, the American critical theorist David Carroll argues that reflective judgement 'cannot be situated in one field, genre, or *regime* alone, but cuts through and makes links among them all. In other words, it is always necessary to judge. Where there are no fixed criteria . . . one must judge, case by case, without criteria' (Carroll 1987: 173). Lyotard himself uses the image of an archipelago to illustrate the importance of reflective judgement. Each island is a genre of discourse, linked to the others by the sea, and judgement is the mode in which one navigates between them:

> Each genre of discourse would be like an island; the faculty of judge-
> ment would be ... like an admiral or like a provisioner of ships who
> would launch expeditions from one island to the next, intended to
> present to one island what was found ... in the other.

(Lyotard 1988a: 130–1)

Continuing this analogy, Lyotard argues that judgement's movement
around the archipelago can link the different genres through trade
and commerce between them or, alternatively, can mount attacks
or challenges through war or piracy. In other words, the genres
(islands) are formed, sustained and allowed to communicate by the
reflective judgements that move between them. Any change in a
genre, and conflict or meeting between genres, is produced by
reflective thought; without reflection, one is stuck within the rules
and structures of a genre just as the community without boats would
be trapped on their island.

Perhaps the clearest way to set out the implications of the differences between determinate and reflective judgement is to return to
the Australian land-rights trial that was described in Chapter 3. Faced
with the women's inability to speak, the judge has two possibilities
for adjudicating in the case. If he or she employs determinate criteria,
he or she will follow the existing precedents set down in law and
will necessarily find in favour of the land developer because the
women hadn't provided evidence. In effect, the judge ignores the
existence of the differend in which the women find themselves and
thereby wrongs them by refusing to hear their speech (or, in effect,
to take account of the importance of their silence). The alternative
for the judge would be to respond reflectively and attempt to seek
out a genre in which the differend between the two parties can be
phrased. Obviously this is not an easy option. All of the judge's
training will be called into question, as well as the legal system of
the country and perhaps its political integrity, and there are no guarantees that any solution satisfactory to all parties will be discovered.
Ethically, however, Lyotard would argue that the judge is obliged to

take the latter course and judge reflectively because to remain within the determinate criteria of the legal system would be to suppress the differend and condemn the women to silence.

Reflective judgement is therefore crucial to Lyotard's thought. In fact, he argues that reflective judgement is the model for postmodern philosophy: 'philosophical discourse obeys a fundamental rule, namely that it must be in search of its rule' (1989: 394). The task of thinking is reflectively to respond to things that happen in order to attempt to discover new rules and modes of acting in the present. This emphasis on reflective judgement brings Lyotard's account of the practice of philosophy particularly close to his analysis of the role of the postmodern work of art or literature, which 'is not in principle governed by pre-established rules and cannot be judged according to determinant judgement, by the application of given categories to this text or work' (1992: 15). Art, as was argued in the last chapter, is a key site from which reflection can emerge. Literary or artistic presentation has the potential to disturb established genres of discourse and, because of its eventhood, challenge hitherto accepted ways of seeing and knowing the world. Approached reflectively, art can surprise us and throw open new possibilities for thinking; however if one approaches art or literature with pre-given critical methods that are simply applied to the works to judge them determinately, what is challenging, surprising and potentially transformative in these works is lost. The postmodern critic, according to Lyotard, must therefore be able to judge reflectively and be open to the work of art's or literature's status as an event.

CULTURE AND CRITICISM

The key reason that Lyotard resorts to reflective judgement arises from his analysis of the structures of contemporary culture and his critique of the grand narratives of modernity. For Lyotard, the thinker or critic cannot be someone who stands outside of the complexities of culture and society and is able to view them in scientific, impartial terms from the position of some ultimately true or just genre of discourse that is capable of organising all other texts, genres and events into a system. All subjects exist as parts of a culture or cultures whose dominant genres of discourse shape the ways in which they perceive the world. In other words, culture is not something that is 'added on' to a pre-established subject or individual, but rather what shapes that individual and makes her or him into a subject. (This is the basis of Lyotard's anti-humanist philosophy of phrases and the differend that was discussed in Chapter 3.) And this is just as true of contemporary culture as it was of cultures in the past. In an early essay called 'Dead Letter' (1962), Lyotard defines culture in the following manner:

> Historically, culture is a particular way of being in fundamental situations: birth, death, love, work, giving birth, being embodied, growing old, speaking. People have to be born, to die, and so forth, and a people arises in response to these tasks, to these calls, as it understands them. This understanding, this listening, and the resonance that is granted it, · is at the same time what a people is, its understanding of itself, its being-together. Culture is not a system of meanings attributed to fundamental situations on the basis of conventions, a project or a contract; it is the being-there that is people.

> (Lyotard 1993c: 33)

A people arise from the ways in which they communally understand those key moments in life such as birth, love and death. These shared understandings are not consciously adopted by individuals in the way one might put on a particular outfit to visit a certain social event, but rather shape the essence of what those people conceive themselves to be and provide the basic structures of the ways in which they interrelate with each other. This is what Lyotard calls culture. In other words, culture is not a secondary rationalisation or explanation of relationships that is added to subjective experience in order to explain how people get on together. Rather, culture is precisely those modes of relating that take place irrespective of whether or not they are understood or formally recognised and made into laws and contracts.

This understanding of what culture is runs throughout Lyotard's writing. It is perhaps most clearly expounded in his discussions of the Cashinahua tribe that was discussed in Chapter 1 (for Lyotard's key discussions of the Cashinahua, see 1984: 20–1; 1985: 32–5; 1988a: 152–5). Here, because of the apparent simplicity of their social organisation, it is relatively easy to see how the construction of the tribe's cultural coherence is generated by their processes of shared storytelling in which their beliefs, identities and relationships are related back to them. Each member of the tribe is located in relation to the narratives (who can tell, who is allowed to listen, who features as a hero, etc.), and the significant events of tribal life (births, deaths, marriages, etc.) that are recounted. In this sense, Cashinahua identity arises from this shared culture constructed in their stories.

In modern capitalist societies, however, this sense of a coherent culture is much more problematic. In 'Dead Letter', Lyotard argues that we are becoming 'cut off' from culture:

> sign and signification, activity and culture, living and understanding are dissociated . . . [In modernity] activities devoid of meaning are organised according to the model of the machine, a model whose purpose lies outside itself, which does not question that purpose. A mechanistic economy, whose principle is the search for an optimal relation between expenditure and production, is imposed as the rule of all activities . . . Working becomes that carrying out of operations, subjected to imperatives of time and even of norms foreign to its content, ultimately decided by the axiom . . . that 'economic' society is a machine and ought to obey the rule of the best possible cost/benefit ratio, for all types of results and investments.
>
> (Lyotard 1993c: 34–5)

This notion of modernity as the gradual encroachment of technology and machines into the realm of human identity should be familiar from discussions of *The Postmodern Condition*, *Libidinal Economy*, *Duchamp's TRANS/formers* and *The Inhuman* in earlier chapters. In each of these texts, Lyotard investigates and questions modernity's modes of relating culture to technology, and works through the implications of capitalism's transformations of human experience in which subjective existence is reduced to just one more aspect of an economic system whose only goal is to maximise profits. The aim of his work, and the reason for its focus on disruption and the differend, is to challenge the reduction of difference to the single criterion of efficiency.

POSTMODERN CRITICISM: REWRITING MODERNITY

As the last chapter argued, this process of dehumanisation in modernity is described in the introduction to *The Inhuman* as a conflict between two forms of the inhuman: on the one hand the inhuman technological system, and on the other the inhuman 'no man's land' at the heart of the subject. In a key essay in that book, called 'Rewriting Modernity', Lyotard begins to explore the ways in which the second sense of the inhuman can be brought into play by the critic to resist the reduction of culture to the calculability of profit and loss in contemporary capitalism.

Lyotard begins the essay by arguing that, 'neither modernity nor so-called postmodernity can be identified and defined as clearly circumscribed historical entities, of which the latter would always come "after" the former. Rather we have to say that the postmodern is always implied in the modern' (1991a: 25). This argument is similar to his analysis of the relation between the modern and the postmodern in 'An Answer to the Question: What is the Postmodern?' that was discussed in Chapter 2. Lyotard refuses to separate the two as historical periods, but rather presents them as different responses to the world and history. His process of distinguishing between these two forms of response in 'Rewriting Modernity' focuses on the different ways in which they engage with the event. The way in which he analyses this difference is through a reading of Sigmund Freud's distinctions between repeating, remembering and working-through.

SIGMUND FREUD (1856–1939)

Freud founded the discourse of psychoanalysis while working in Vienna at the end of the nineteenth century. His practice explored the processes of mental life, and his writings put forward the idea that human consciousness is supplemented by an unconscious that (although we cannot directly experience it consciously) has a huge influence on our desires, motivations and interactions in everyday existence. The unconscious, he argues, is a repository for all of those thoughts and impulses that are too disturbing for conscious reflection and are thus repressed by the mind. Once repressed, however, they do not cease to have affects; rather, their attempts to find their way into consciousness are the basis of the psychological problems that many people face. He therefore developed the techniques of psychoanalysis, often called the 'talking cure', in which patients are helped to come to terms with their illnesses by talking to a psychoanalyst about their lives and attempting to lay to rest the problems caused by repressed desires. This groundbreaking set of arguments transformed many of the ways in which pre-twentieth-century thinkers had conceived of human life, and has been hugely important for philosophy, sociology, psychology and art for the past hundred years. Perhaps the most influential book Freud published was *The Interpretation of Dreams* (1900), but his analyses of mental life led him to discuss subjects as diverse as jokes, Christianity, war, sex and telepathy.

In an important essay from 1914 called 'Remembering, Repeating and Working-Through', Freud explains the place that each of the terms in the title occupies in psychoanalytic theory and practice. Very briefly, repetition arises when repressed thoughts come back to haunt the subject and cause her or him compulsively to repeat an action. So, to take an example from literature, Lady Macbeth's compulsive washing of her hands during the sleepwalking scene in *Macbeth* might indicate to a psychoanalytically inclined reader that the repressed horror of her involvement in King Duncan's murder forces her to repeat an action linked with it. Freud's first idea of the task of the analyst is that he or she should help the patient to remember the repressed event that is causing the repetition. Through remembering what had been repressed, the early Freud thought that the patient might be able to understand and cope with it. He says that when he first began practising psychoanalysis, this was the procedure he followed. However, he claims that more recent experience has shown him that such remembering is sometimes not possible, and that even when it is it might not have the desired effect of curing the patient. He therefore introduced the process of what he calls 'working through'. Here, rather than bringing the original traumatic event back into consciousness, psychoanalysis consists in working on the repetition itself in order to trace out its range of meanings and associations and, to put it simply, come to terms with it. The original trauma is never fully defined (Freud argues that such a definition might be impossible), but its negative effects are, as far as possible, neutralised. In working through there is a process of continual adjustment of associations and memories and this implies, as Freud argues in another essay, that the process of analysis is 'interminable' — it is never completed.

Lyotard picks up on the distinction between remembering and working through in order to describe the different approaches of a modern and a postmodern critic. A modern critic, he argues, 'wants to remember, to gather up the dismembered temporality [of the event] that has not been mastered . . . Like in a detective novel, the case is examined, witnesses called, information gathered' (1991a: 27). What Lyotard draws from Freud's account of remembering, then, is that the analyst brings the event that is remembered into an explanatory discourse: it is 'mastered' by analysis and, like a crime in detective fiction, its ambiguities and the problems it throws up are solved. With regard to the modern thinker or critic, this means that the event or text that is being analysed is provided with an apparently complete explanation as it is fitted into a particular genre of discourse and 'made sense of'. The example Lyotard gives of this approach is the Marxist analysis of capitalism in which Marx 'detects the hidden functioning of capitalism' and, having discovered this, 'believes he has identified and denounced the original crime from which is born the unhappiness of modernity: the exploitation of the workers. And like a detective he imagines that by revealing "reality" – i.e. liberal society and economics – as a fraud, he is allowing humanity to escape its great plague' (1991a: 28). A Marxist analysis is modern because, as Lyotard argues, in 'detecting the crime' of capitalist economics, it provides an answer to society's problems and, from this, develops an alternative account of the future as a utopian socialist community. In other words, it sets up its own, alternative, grand narrative.

For Lyotard, postmodern criticism would focus much more clearly on the Freudian notion of working-through: 'contrary to remembering, working through would be defined as a work without end . . . in the sense in which it is not guided by the concept of an end' (1991a: 30). This means that a critical engagement with the event must remain open instead of already being guided by an established genre of discourse that has particular ends (the freedom of the workers, for example) in mind from the beginning. It is thus never 'complete' as the event has not been (and as the last chapter argued, cannot be) explained in its entirety but has, instead, been opened up to a series of possible thoughts and responses. In this way, Lyotard argues that working through is 'attached to a thought of what is constitutively hidden from us in the event and the meaning of the event, hidden not merely by past prejudice, but also by those dimensions of the future marked out by the pro-ject' (1991a: 26). The task of the postmodern critic is thus not to 'explain' the event, but rather to pay attention to it and respond to it in such a way that it retains its singularity but can be brought to bear to challenge the certainties and truths presented by the modern thinker, possibly even to demonstrate the violence and suffering inherent in modernity's projects. His key example of this process is the events connected under the name of Auschwitz that were discussed in Chapter 4.

Acknowledging her or his place in a culture that is already guided by genres of discourse and the grand narratives of modernity, the critic's task is to uncover events that are suppressed in these genres and narratives and open them up for investigation. This investigation is, in its turn, reflective: the task of criticism is to bear witness to the surprise of the event and not silence the possibility of its differend by explaining it in terms of established modes of knowledge. In this sense, the critic's attempts to work through modernity are interminable as there is no simple or quick resolution of the meaning of a text or event, but rather openness to its problematisation of realist presentation. Lyotard sums this process up in the following passage:

> in working through, the only guiding thread at one's disposal consists in sentiment or, better still, in listening to a sentiment. A fragment of a sentence, a scrap of information, a word, come along . . . By proceeding in this way, one slowly approaches a scene, the scene of something. One describes it. One does not know what it is. One is sure only that it refers to some past, both furthest and nearest past, both one's own past and others' past. This lost time is not represented like a picture, it is not even presented. It is what presents the elements of a picture, an impossible picture. Rewriting means registering these elements.
>
> (1991a: 31)

Rewriting, like working through, is thus an interminable task. Judging events in a postmodern, reflective manner always leaves them open to further analysis and discussion rather than 'solving' them by finding the 'truth' and thereby erecting one's own analysis as a new grand narrative. This seemingly never-ending process of rewriting modernity is, again, best exemplified in literary criticism. The fact that one has read or seen *Hamlet* does not make it a waste of time to read or see it again. No reading of the play is either fixed or final. Rereading will always throw up more and different ideas and impressions for thinking about both the play and the world. Each rereading will have different points of focus, debate and impact, and hence open possibilities for different ideas of politics and culture. *Hamlet* does not have a singular fixed meaning which the critic's aim is to pin down once and for all. Rather, the play contains a vast range of meanings, ideas, implications and events that are available for analysis, discussion and argument, and which open up ways of working through the genres of the modernity of which it forms a part. To read any work of art or literature is, for Lyotard, to engage with the culture from which it comes (as well as one's own contemporary culture) in ways that seek to uncover events, signs and differends and open them up to critical thought.

MALRAUX AND THE REWRITING OF MODERNITY

Two of Lyotard's last books serve as a helpful example of how he puts the ideas of culture, modernity and judgement to work in his own writing. These books, *Signed Malraux* (1996) and *Soundproof Room: Malraux's Anti-Aesthetics* (1998), discuss the life and work of the French adventurer, artist and thinker, André Malraux.

Signed Malraux can be read as a biography: Lyotard's discussions explore French society through the relations between the thought, artistic practice, politics and life of Malraux. It is not a standard biography, however. As Lyotard declares at the outset, his readings of Malraux's writing 'fictionally constructs this putative "life". What is authentic is not what some third party verifies or confesses, but what this "life" signs' (1999: 11). In other words, this is less a biography than a distillation of a character, the signatory 'Malraux', from writings by him. It is a fiction, or rather a 'myth', that constructs the life and world of the writer from the narratives presented in his works. These writings thus provide the symptoms, signs and events within modernity that Lyotard's book works through.

From this basis, Lyotard sketches out the story of Malraux's life from his childhood, through his career as smuggler, antifascist airman in the Spanish Civil War, fighter with the French Resistance in the Second World War, representative of the post-war French government, artist, thinker and writer. In Lyotard's hands, these incidents become more than anecdotes from a life: they are a means of entry into many of the complex philosophical, cultural and political problems faced by modernity. No single 'André Malraux' emerges (or is remembered in the modern manner). Instead, Lyotard's working-through of the events of his writings produces a multiplicity of 'Malrauxs' that intersect with and question different discourses of modernity.

Soundproof Room focuses much more explicitly on the role of literature in this process of rewriting modernity. Through discussions of Malraux's novels and their relations to currents in twentieth-century thought, Lyotard works through in some detail literature's potential impact on a range of modernity's motifs and examines its potential for political and philosophical disruption. In a key passage, he argues that

> the artwork never gets clear of anything, never exceeds its subjection to the world. It is a first step beyond, the beginning of an entry into the desert: the exodus out of the sensual Egypt is not and must not be accomplished. Style relentlessly works, undoing and reshaping its material in order to snatch it from the spiral of the sensible, to subvert and offer it up to the call of the unheard-of. Yet style firmly maintains sounds, words, colours, all the timbres from which it composes the artwork

within their material element. And the forms that it invents for them and which it imposes on reality will not be emancipated from reality: to it they *promise* escape.

(2001: 98–100)

This is perhaps the clearest summary of the place of art and literature that Lyotard provides. Works of art are parts of the world from which they emerge. They do not descend from a higher realm or appear from the individual genius of an artist. And, equally, they do not permit an escape from the world to some 'Promised Land' of imaginative reconciliation. As part of the world, however, the work's formal reshaping of the material elements that make it up have the potential to point to the limitedness of that world and to project, to 'promise', the possibility of an escape into a transformed world, to hold out a future that differs from the constraints of the present. This is what makes the work of art an event, and what forms the point of departure for a criticism that seeks to grasp its political potential to challenge the assumed, everyday ways of thinking and acting of a culture or genre of discourse. No real future resolution is presented, but the present systems of rationality are shaken: the work presents that there is an unpresentable in every presentation, and the critical thinker's task is to respond to the implications of that unpresentable in ways that challenge those genres and systems that have served to occlude its very existence.

SUMMARY

Lyotard's work across a range of areas from art and literature to history and politics seeks out the moments at which what he is discussing reveals the potential to disrupt the genres of discourse from which it appears to emerge. Because of his focus on figures such as the sublime, the differend, the sign and the event, Lyotard does not offer a system or programme for thought or action. Rather, he urges the critic actively to question such programmes and investigate what they exclude or silence.

Lyotard's work thus offers a range of possibilities for the critical thinker to employ in her or his analyses of modernity. It is not a question of escaping into some sort of postmodern utopia. Instead Lyotard argues that the critic's task is interminably to rewrite modernity in order to expose the moments where the genres of discourse that make up grand narratives are opened to question and the possibility of change emerges. Lyotard's last works provide excellent if complex demonstrations of these processes of rewriting through analyses of the work of André Malraux.

AFTER LYOTARD

Lyotard's writing has had a major impact on work across the Humanities. His most influential text, *The Postmodern Condition*, has become a standard reference point for the discussion of postmodernity in Literary Studies, Philosophy, Sociology and Politics, as well as newer disciplines such as Cultural Theory and Media Studies. In effect, no study of the postmodern is complete without reference to this or other of Lyotard's texts. Many of these other works have also appealed to more specialist audiences in the Humanities, and these too have challenged traditional approaches to literature, culture, philosophy and politics in a number of fields.

The question of the precise extent of Lyotard's influence, however, is slightly more difficult to gauge. Because, as the last chapter tried to demonstrate, he did not erect a critical system that could be applied at will by anyone who has studied his work in order to explain texts or events, responses to his writings have tended to engage with his arguments and take certain of his ideas for use in other media while not following some of the wider implications of his analyses. It seems that there are few card-carrying Lyotardians working in the Humanities today, and yet this is certainly not to say that his ideas are not important or influential. Lyotard's categories and modes of argument appear in a wide range of different critical thinkers' analyses of contemporary culture, including those whose political or philosophical positions appear to be distinctly at odds with his own. In fact, those thinkers who disagree with Lyotard often provide more interesting and nuanced readings of his work than those who attempt simply to 'apply' ideas like the sublime or the differend to other texts. Lyotard's engagements with a wide range of the most important and influential figures in the history of Western thought such as Kant, Augustine, Hegel, Freud and Marx have frequently resulted in readings that have been adopted by the scholarly communities that have grown up around those writers, and remain central texts in those areas. Moreover, terms such as the sublime, the event and the differend that Lyotard has recovered or developed frequently appear in contexts where he is not the subject of explicit discussion, and may barely even be mentioned. It would be fair to say, however, that there are three main areas where Lyotard's work is currently being explored and expanded upon. These are the postmodern, the inhuman and aesthetics. Each of these will be discussed in more detail in the paragraphs below, and details will be given of some of the critics who have responded to Lyotard's writing in these areas.

Since the publication of *The Postmodern Condition*, discussions of postmodernism and postmodernity have multiplied rapidly across the Humanities. As this book has attempted to demonstrate, Lyotard's influence in this area has been vast. His definition of the postmodern as an 'incredulity toward metanarratives' (1984: xxiv) has become one of the most frequently quoted definitions of the post-modern condition – even if it has often been misunderstood or misused. Along with Fredric Jameson and Jean Baudrillard, critics regularly cite him as a founding thinker of postmodern critical theory. As Chapter 4 argued, however, each of these writers con-structs a very different account of postmodernism, and each has influenced different areas of enquiry and worked to different ends.

Because of the range and detail of Lyotard's work, it is problematic to assign him a specific type of postmodernism or limit his influence to a particular sphere. Broadly speaking, however, one might argue that those approaches that take the postmodern as a philosophical problem or a positive political challenge to established ways of explaining human culture tend to cite Lyotard as their key influence.

Too many writers have drawn upon Lyotard's work on the post-modern to list them all here, but some of the most widely influential engagements with a Lyotardian notion of postmodernity in the areas of Politics, History and Cultural and Literary Studies include the following texts. A very good general discussion of postmodern culture and society can be found in David Harvey's *The Condition of Postmodernity* (1990), which has become one of the standard analyses of postmodernity, even if its readings of Lyotard are somewhat reductive and not always entirely helpful. Harvey treats the post-modern as more than just a cultural phenomenon, mining Western thought from the Enlightenment to the present in order to investigate the transformations that have taken place in the meaning and perception of time and space during this period, and the effect of these transformations on the ways in which we experience society and culture. Although he cites only *The Postmodern Condition* (and in a slightly disparaging way), Harvey's analysis of the postmodern bears a much closer resemblance to Lyotard's investigation of genres of discourse and signs of history in *The Differend*, and could quite helpfully be read alongside that book.

For those interested in history and the postmodern, an excellent discussion that draws heavily on the work of Lyotard and Baudrillard to challenge traditional practices of writing history is Keith Jenkins' *Why History? Ethics and Postmodernity* (1999). For Jenkins, the idea of an 'end of history' should be understood in a double sense: not only does postmodernism mark the end of history as a grand narrative of Marxist or liberal progress, but it also attacks history as it has been, and frequently still is, practised by academic historians in Britain and North America. Lyotard is a key source for this challenge to academic history, and Jenkins' readings of *The Postmodern Condition* and Lyotard's essays on history are not only helpful introductions, but also important demonstrations of the challenges that his work lays down to established disciplinary procedures.

In literary criticism, there have been many different attempts to rework Lyotard's ideas. One of the most successful writers in this endeavour, and certainly one of the most helpful for students of contemporary literature, is the Canadian critic Linda Hutcheon whose *A Poetics of Postmodernism* (1988) and *The Politics of Postmodernism* (1989) both provide detailed analyses of a vast range of postmodern literature and culture with reference to many of Lyotard's ideas about history, the sublime and politics. Rather than providing detailed investigations of Lyotard's work, Hutcheon focuses on the transformations that have taken place in literature and culture since the Second World War (thereby presenting the postmodern as a historical period set against literary modernism in a way Lyotard would not) to provide a series of analyses of art's potential to engage with broader social issues. A key aspect of Hutcheon's work is her discussion of postmodernism and its relation to recent attempts by feminist critics to rethink and challenge patriarchal ideas of gender, and she adopts Lyotard's writing as a key component of her critical approach to this problem. Another important analysis of Lyotard's value for gender studies can be found in the American critic Alice Jardine's complex book, *Gynesis: Configurations of Woman and Modernity* (1985), which discusses Lyotard's value for contemporary feminist theory in detail.

The second broad area where Lyotard's work has proved to be influential can be called 'the inhuman'. There is an increasing interest about the relations between human and machine consciousness in the Humanities, as well as a growing body of work on what it means to be human in the contemporary world that challenges the Enlightenment ideas of humanism and universal humanity. Much of this work draws on Lyotard's analyses of culture and politics, particularly in *The Differend* and *The Inhuman*, in order to 'think the limits of the human' as it appears in contemporary culture. As Chapters 3 and 5 argued, Lyotard's critical thinking sets out to problematise humanism through his philosophies of phrases, the sublime and the differend, and this critique has been taken up by a number of thinkers as a means of working through the impacts that developments in technology and science have had on our sense of what it means to be human at the beginning of the twenty-first century.

The most straightforward introduction to this work is a short book by Stuart Sim entitled *Lyotard and the Inhuman* (2001), which reads Lyotard's discussions of the inhuman and postmodernity in relation to other thinkers' analyses of cyborgs, the Internet and artificial intelligence. For Sim, Lyotard's arguments in *The Inhuman* about the encroachment of technological criteria into all aspects of life and the concomitant destruction of humanism provide a point of departure from which one can begin to understand the impact of the development of communication technologies such as the Internet and artificial intelligence. His reading of Lyotard is astute, and this book helpfully opens a field of study that is rapidly gaining importance in the Humanities.

A more complex and philosophically exploratory discussion is provided in the essays collected by Scott Brewster, John Joughin, David Owen and Richard Walker in a book entitled *Inhuman Reflections: Thinking the Limits of the Human* (2000). This fascinating collection draws heavily on Lyotard's work to think through the relationships obtaining between the inhuman, modernity, literature, desire and the future. Lyotard's thought is referred to throughout this book, which also includes a particularly astute analysis of his work, from *Libidinal Economy* to *Heidegger and 'the jews'*, by Gary Banham. What the writers here gesture towards is the importance for contemporary cultural criticism of Lyotard's second sense of the inhuman – that which within the human resists reduction either to humanism or to the various techno-scientific systems that have come to supplant it. Another very helpful collection of essays, which also deal with Lyotard's thought and includes an extract reprinted from *The Inhuman*, is

Posthumanism (2000), edited by Neil Badmington. This book collects some of the key contributions to this area of study and reproduces them with clear and helpful introductory notes for students.

In the light of Lyotard's analyses of art and the sublime which have been discussed at length in this book, it is worth pointing to a third area where Lyotard's work continues to be developed. This area is the aesthetic. There is a growing interest in the philosophical, literary and political importance of aesthetics, and Lyotard's work in this area has been hugely influential: the sublime has, in recent years, become one of the key categories of critical investigation, and Lyotard's readings of the place of sublimity in Kant, Hegel and in the eighteenth-century Irish critic, Edmund Burke, have become key points of reference for those wanting to explore the political and philosophical impact of this figure in contemporary culture.

The key book for students wanting to find out more about Lyotard's impact on these contemporary discussions of aesthetics is *Paraesthetics: Foucault, Lyotard, Derrida* (1987) by David Carroll. This text explores the ways in which Lyotard's conception of aesthetics gives rise to his political analyses of postmodern culture, and Carroll's clear and detailed analyses produce some important insights into Lyotard's philosophy. Helpfully, it links his work not just with preceding philosophers and critics, but also with two of the other important contemporary French writers, Michel Foucault and Jacques Derrida, to give a sense of the range of current theoretical interest in aesthetics.

A much more complex, but nevertheless very important, collection of essays by an even wider range of the leading contemporary French thinkers (which includes an original essay by Lyotard) is translated into English by Jeffrey Librett with the title *Of the Sublime: Presence in Question* (1993). Many of these essays draw heavily on Lyotard's work to explore the importance of the sublime in the history of philosophy and also for the politics of modern art, literature and culture. The pieces collected here are often very difficult and require some specialist philosophical knowledge, but for readers who are prepared to persevere this book presents a picture both of where critical analysis of aesthetics is heading, and also of Lyotard's importance for this project.

Recently, critics working in English Studies have begun to pick up on the importance of aesthetics. A key publication in this developing field is Terry Eagleton's *The Ideology of the Aesthetic* (1990), which explores the development of aesthetics from the eighteenth century to the present in a clear and lucid style, even if its reading of Lyotard is somewhat negative. Eagleton explores the politics of different ideas of the aesthetic from Kant to the postmodernists, arguing that it is both tied up with ideology and politics, and yet is also capable of generating the means to critique social systems and values. *The Radical Aesthetic* (2000) by Isobel Armstrong also investigates the importance of a consideration of the aesthetic for literary and cultural criticism, and is much more positive about Lyotard and other postmodern descriptions of aesthetics than Eagleton. In both Eagleton's and Armstrong's books, however, the aesthetic is used as a means to raise questions about the political and organisational systems of the modern world, and their processes of questioning the different constructions of the aesthetic bear a number of similarities with Lyotard's notion of rewriting modernity that was introduced in Chapter 6.

Since his death in 1998, Lyotard's importance has continued to grow as critics have returned to his work in order to find new ways to think through some of the most complex and pressing problems faced by contemporary society. As more of his works are translated into English, the questions addressed in his thought have become wider, and the influence of his probing analyses of politics, philosophy, art and culture has spread throughout the Humanities. It is too early to judge the full extent of this influence, and difficult to predict the areas into which critics and thinkers will draw Lyotard's versatile thought in the future. What can be ascertained, however, is that the challenges laid out in his work will remain vitally important for anyone wishing to understand the contemporary world for some time to come.

FURTHER READING

WORKS BY JEAN-FRANÇOIS LYOTARD

All of the texts discussed in this book are available in English translation, as the majority of Lyotard's works now are. Most students first encounter Lyotard's ideas through such books and articles as *The Postmodern Condition* or 'An Answer to the Question: What is the Postmodern?'. These are probably the best places to begin to get a sense of Lyotard's critical thought, but they are far from representative of its full range. From these it is possible to move on to *Just Gaming*, which engages with many of the issues raised in those two texts in the open and accessible manner of a series of recorded interviews, and *The Differend*, which is perhaps his most important work and provides the most detailed way in to the complexities of Lyotard's later writings. Some readers will, of course, want to explore Lyotard's earlier work, and the most readily available text for this is probably *Libidinal Economy*. This is a very difficult and sometimes disturbing book, but one that is continually fascinating and the focus of growing critical interest. Readers might also be drawn towards Lyotard's shorter critical essays, and these appear in a number of helpful collections including *The Postmodern Explained*, *The Inhuman*, *Political Writings*, *Postmodern Fables* and the *Lyotard Reader*. Each of these collections contains useful selections from his work in many of the areas discussed in this book. Fuller details of all of these texts are given below.

This book has focused predominantly on texts written by Lyotard from the late 1970s to the present, which might be called his 'post-modern' works. However, there are a number of other important pieces that there has not been the space to examine here. As well as the books that have been discussed, these others are listed below with brief descriptions of their content, importance and accessibility for students.

In this section, Lyotard's works are ordered by their original publication date, to give an idea of his publishing career. With the exception of those collections of essays that have been produced and translated especially for an English-speaking audience, all of the works listed originally appeared in French. The publication details here indicate the English versions that you will be most likely to consult. For this reason, two dates appear in most of the references: the first, in square brackets, is the original publication date, while the second date and all other details refer to the translation. If only one date appears, this means the text or collection was originally published in English.

—— [1954] (1991) *Phenomenology*, trans. B. Bleakley, Albany, New York: State University of New York Press.

This was Lyotard's first book. It discusses the value of phenom-enology (a form of philosophical analysis) for various aspects of the human sciences, and particularly in relation to Marxism. There are a range of important arguments in this book, and much that surfaces again in Lyotard's later work. However, because of its detailed philosophical discussions, its main interest will probably be to those readers concerned with Lyotard's relation to the history of philosophy.

—— [1974] (1993) *Libidinal Economy*, trans. Iain Hamilton Grant, London: Athlone.

This is probably Lyotard's most important and challenging early work that is available in English translation. This is a very difficult but continually stimulating text, which provides some fascinating discussions of Freud, Marx and capitalism. Lyotard's long and complex sentences are sometimes very hard to follow, but the images he employs are frequently arresting and thought provoking. Often disturbing, this text is generating increasing interest among critics and thinkers who are paying more attention to work that precedes his interest in the postmodern. A particularly good exposition of this book is given in James Williams, *Lyotard and the Political* (2000).

—— [1977] (1990) *Duchamp's TRANS/formers*, Venice, California: Lapis Press.

This book collects a series of essays and lectures in which Lyotard attempts to analyse the work of the twentieth-century experimental artist, Marcel Duchamp. Playful and often amusing, Lyotard draws on ideas generated in *Libidinal Economy* and other early works to illustrate the challenges Duchamp's work poses to contemporary thought and society.

—— [1979] (1984) *The Postmodern Condition: A Report on Knowledge*, trans. Geoff Bennington and Brian Massumi, Manchester: Manchester University Press.

This was the book that first made Lyotard widely known in the English-speaking world, and remains his most discussed text. Although it is not necessarily representative of his work as a whole, the postmodern is the theme that is most readily associated with his writing. Commissioned by the government of Quebec, Lyotard produced a report on the state of knowledge in contemporary western societies, which argues that the grand narratives that shaped modernity are no longer credible and new means of comprehending the world have become necessary. This was a groundbreaking work, and still provides one of the most incisive descriptions of post-modernity available. Because it is a text that is so widely known, it is probably the best place to begin reading Lyotard. Appended to the English translation of *The Postmodern Condition* is his important essay, 'Answering the Question: What is Postmodernism?' A more helpful translation of this essay is, however, included in *The Postmodern Explained* (1992).

—— with Jean-Loup Thébaud [1979] (1985) *Just Gaming*, trans. Wlad Godzich, Minneapolis: University of Minnesota Press.

This is a key text, which is discussed in more detail in Chapter 3. First published in French in the same year as *The Postmodern Condition* (1979), this book is made up of a series of discussions between Lyotard and Jean-Loup Thébaud about ethics, politics and whether it is possible to have a workable conception of justice in postmodernity. The discussions are wide ranging, and touch on many important aspects of Lyotard's thought as Thébaud's questions carefully probe for inconsistencies and contradictions. Although some of the arguments might appear somewhat obscure to the non-philosophical reader, the clarity and sense of adventure in this text makes it an absorbing and rewarding read.

—— [1983] (1988) *The Differend: Phrases in Dispute*, trans. Georges Van Den Abeele, Manchester: Manchester University Press.

This is probably Lyotard's most important and far-reaching book. In *The Differend*, Lyotard develops the discussion of language games presented in *The Postmodern Condition* and *Just Gaming* to generate a much more versatile philosophy of phrases. The book includes analyses of the Holocaust, modernity, ethics, history and politics, all of which are discussed in relation to his notion of a differend in which alternative ways of phrasing are silenced or excluded by mainstream genres of discourse. *The Differend* provides the theoretical under-pinning for much of Lyotard's later work and has had a huge impact across the Humanities. This is a central text that any serious critic of Lyotard must engage with. It is also fascinating to read.

—— [1984] (1998) *The Assassination of Exp[...] Monory*, trans. Rachel Bowlby, London: Black Do[...]

In his analysis of the French artist, Jacques Mo[...] Lyotard discusses two series of paintings in great detail, [...] are included as black and white or colour illustrations in [...]. The book was written over a long period and, consequently, [...]monstrates the changes and continuities between his work in texts such as *Libidinal Economy* and *The Differend*. This is probably the best example in English of Lyotard's approach to fine art, and also contains a good deal of material that picks up on his more well-known texts on the postmodern. It is a very good example of the complex ways in which Lyotard approaches art in the light of a range of social, political and philosophical questions.

—— (1988) *Peregrinations: Law, Form, Event* New York: Columbia University Press.

This book developed from a series of three lectures in which Lyotard describes his development as a thinker and discusses some of the implications of his work for analysing the contemporary world. It also includes a long essay, entitled 'A Memorial for Marxism', in which he gives details of his break with the Marxist revolutionary movement, *Socialisme ou Barbarie*. The book ends with a very detailed bibliography of Lyotard's work and critical responses to it up until 1987. Because of the clarity of the writing and sometimes informal style of the delivery, this is one of the best introductions to Lyotard's work.

—— [1988] (1992) *The Postmodern Explained: Correspondence 1982– 1985*, trans. Don Barry, Bernadette Maher, Julian Pefanis, Virginia Spate and Morgan Thomas, Minneapolis: University of Minnesota Press.

This is a collection of very important and influential essays written by Lyotard in response to the debates that followed his publication of *The Postmodern Condition*. The essays provide some very useful links between that book and *The Differend*, and helpfully expand upon ideas

...ssed in both. The book includes central essays such as 'An Answer to the Question: What is the Postmodern?', 'Missive on Universal History', 'Note on the Meaning of the "Post-"' and 'Gloss on Resistance', as well as a number of others, all in excellently accurate and clear translations. This is one of the best texts to move on to after reading *The Postmodern Condition*.

Another edition of this has been released as *The Postmodern Explained to Children: Correspondence 1982–1985* (London: Turnaround, 1992), which is identical in all respects except that it does not contain the final explanatory essay written by the critic Wlad Godzich.

—— [1988] (1990) *Heidegger and 'the jews'*, trans. Andreas Michel and Mark Roberts, Minneapolis: University of Minnesota Press.

This book focuses on a key intellectual crisis in French thought: the revelation that one of their key sources, the German philosopher Martin Heidegger, had been both a sympathiser with and a member of the Nazi Party. In the light of his discussions of the Holocaust in texts including *The Differend*, Lyotard contributes to the debate about Heidegger's Nazism. The first section in the book discusses the place of 'the jews' (presented in lower case and inverted commas as a representative of the outsider) in Western culture, and returns to questions about the Holocaust and history. The second section discusses Heidegger, and while refusing to condone his relation to Nazism, attempts to think through its implications for contemporary theory. This is a complex book that draws on ideas developed in *The Differend*, and is probably best read in the light of the arguments there.

—— [1988] (1991) *The Inhuman: Reflections on Time*, trans. Geoffrey Bennington and Rachel Bowlby, Cambridge: Polity Press.

The Inhuman is one of Lyotard's most important and wide-ranging books. In effect a collection of essays, this text examines a range of issues from modern art to technological innovation in terms of the way in which they are related to time. This text contains a number of essays such as 'Rewriting Modernity' and 'The Sublime and the

Avant Garde' in which some of Lyotard's most radical and important ideas are developed. It is probably best read in the light of Lyotard's discussions in *The Differend* as it employs many of the ideas developed there, but, because of its lucidity, it should still be accessible to readers not familiar with the earlier text.

—— (1989) *The Lyotard Reader*, Andrew Benjamin (ed.), Oxford: Blackwell.

This is an important collection of some of Lyotard's key essays from a range of moments in his career. The book includes some of Lyotard's most influential analyses of art (including the discussion of Barnett Newman from *The Inhuman* cited in Chapter 5), psychoanalysis, film and Judaism. The final essays on history and the Holocaust are crucial for an understanding of Lyotard's politics.

—— [1991] (1994) *Lessons on the Analytic of the Sublime*, trans. Elizabeth Rottenberg, Stanford, California: Stanford University Press.

In this book Lyotard provides a detailed reading of Immanuel Kant's description of the sublime in the *Critique of Judgement*. Although certainly of interest to students of Philosophy, this text will be useful for anybody wanting a more detailed discussion of Lyotard's notion of the sublime that is central to such key texts as 'An Answer to the Question', *The Differend* and *The Inhuman*. This is quite a complex text and familiarity with Kant's work is helpful, but because Lyotard's explication is so detailed and lucid it is still accessible for the non-philosopher.

—— [1993] (1997) *Postmodern Fables*, trans. Georges Van Den Abeele, Minneapolis: University of Minnesota Press.

This is a collection of essays discussing politics, philosophy, art and culture in the contemporary world. The texts often begin as a short stories or anecdotes, which are then discussed by Lyotard to point towards their wider importance. Because they are frequently amusing to read, these short pieces are probably a good place to encounter some of the complex ideas that Lyotard analyses in more detail in other works. The essay, 'A Postmodern Fable', will be of particular interest to those working on postmodernism.

—— (1993) *Toward the Postmodern*, Robert Harvey and Mark S. Roberts (eds.), New Jersey: Humanities Press.

This is a collection of essays on art, culture and literature written by Lyotard between 1970 and 1991. They include work leading up to and following his opening engagements with the postmodern. A range of discussions are included, some of which are germane to ideas introduced in this book. As they are sometimes quite complex, however, these essays are perhaps best read after becoming familiar with some of Lyotard key texts.

—— (1993) *Political Writings*, trans. Bill Readings and Kevin Paul Geiman, London: University College London Press.

This is a very important collection of essays that cover key ideas raised throughout Lyotard's career from the 1940s to the early 1990s. The focus is on his analyses of political issues, and the essays are organised around themes such as the role of the intellectual, the place of the university in society, the media and the Holocaust. The final section collects some of the essays written by Lyotard during his time as a political activist in Algeria with *Socialisme ou Barbarie*. The range of styles (from television appearances to newspaper articles and seminars) demonstrate the range of Lyotard's work, but makes some more immediately accessible for the beginning reader than others.

—— with Eberhard Gruber [1993] (1999) *The Hyphen: Between Judaism and Christianity*, trans. Pascale-Anne Brault and Michael Nass, New York: Humanity Books.

This text is devoted to a discussion between Lyotard and the critic, Eberhard Gruber, about the meaning of the hyphen in the term 'Judeo-Christian'. The relation between these two religions, both thinkers argue, has shaped some of the key movements in

Western thought and culture from the fall of the Roman Empire to the Nazi Holocaust. Because the centre of their disagreement lies in the fact that Lyotard sees the hyphen as a mark of the presence of a differend between the two terms and Gruber sees it as indicating a passage, this text provides a very good illustration of the sort of issues at stake in Lyotard's notion of the differend. Although philosophically and theologically quite complex in places, it is also a fascinating discussion in its own right.

—— [1996] (1999) *Signed, Malraux*, trans. Robert Harvey, Minneapolis: University of Minnesota Press.

This text presents a biographical account of the French writer and adventurer, André Malraux. It uses his writings, both literary and non-literary, to engage with various aspects of the politics and culture of twentieth-century France, and in particular its colonial rule of Vietnam, the Second World War and the post-war reconstruction of the country. Through this, Lyotard is able to open a series of challenging questions about identity, gender and aesthetics, and he uses Malraux's work to offer some challenges to established ways of theorising these topics. It is a highly enjoyable text to read, and a good place to go in order to see some of the arguments presented in his more abstractly philosophical works put into practice in a specific context.

—— [1998] (2000) *The Confession of Augustine*, trans. Richard Beardsworth, Stanford, California: Stanford University Press.

This is Lyotard's last book, the one he was working on when he died. As a result it remains unfinished, but the fragments collected together in the volume are no less fascinating for that. The text analyses Augustine's *Confessions* (400), and posits it as one of the key source texts for Western modernity because of the way it begins to construct a sense of an individual selfhood. The focus on sexuality, discontinuity and disruption in the book make it an outstanding example of Lyotard's process of 'rewriting modernity' that was discussed in Chapter 6.

—— [1998] (2001) *Soundproof Room: Malraux's Anti-Aesthetics*, trans. Robert Harvey, Stanford, California: Stanford University Press.

This is another of Lyotard's texts that engages with André Malraux. *Soundproof Room* reads Malraux's work in relation to the destruction of modernity's grand narratives and the power generated from the refusal to submit to despair. The book presents a series of important discussions of aesthetics, identity and community, which makes this another extremely important example of what is at stake in Lyotard's project of rewriting modernity.

WORKS ON JEAN-FRANÇOIS LYOTARD

This book is probably the most straightforward critical introduction to Lyotard's work. For those wishing to pursue certain aspects of his writing further, or to focus more specifically on his earlier writings the following texts will probably be the most useful places to begin. Because of the controversial nature of Lyotard's work, critics tend to take a particular stand in relation to his writing. Broadly speaking, those sympathetic to Lyotard's project would include Bennington (1988), Carroll (1987), Readings (1991) and Sim (1996), while those with less sympathy might include Browning (2000) and, at least with respect to Lyotard's postmodern work, Williams (1998 and 2000). The commentary provides brief details about the focus and level of complexity of the texts.

Benjamin, Andrew (ed.) (1992) *Judging Lyotard*, London: Routledge.

This is an excellent collection of essays by mainly British and North American writers on Lyotard's postmodern work, and in particular *The Postmodern Condition* and *Just Gaming*. Although often complex and philosophically sophisticated, the essays here are very helpful in drawing out the arguments presented in Lyotard's critiques of society and politics. This book also contains a translation of an important essay by Lyotard on the politics of Kant's aesthetics, entitled '*Sensus Communis*'.

Bennington, Geoffrey (1988) *Lyotard: Writing the Event*, Manchester: Manchester University Press.

This is an excellent introduction to Lyotard's work from its beginning up until the late 1980s. Bennington writes fluently, while drawing out many of the intricacies of Lyotard's arguments. The main focus of the text is the political implications of the 'event', and the ways in which these politics alter as Lyotard's work develops. Although it moves quite quickly in places, this is a very useful secondary text.

Browning, Gary (2000) *Lyotard and the End of Grand Narratives*, Cardiff: University of Wales Press.

Browning focuses on Lyotard's postmodern challenges to the legitimating grand narratives of modernity. The book offers a helpful overview of his work, and levels a series of important criticisms at it, eventually coming down on the side of a more Marxist/Hegelian line than Lyotard's postmodern thought would support. The focus here is very much on political theory, and it would make a useful background text for students of Sociology or Politics.

Carroll, David (1987) *Paraesthetics: Foucault, Lyotard, Derrida*, London: Methuen.

This book focuses on the importance of aesthetics in the work of Lyotard, as well as in the work of his contemporaries, Jacques Derrida (1930–) and Michel Foucault (1926–84). With regard to Lyotard, Carroll's discussion focuses predominantly on ideas developed in *The Differend*, *Libidinal Economy* and *Just Gaming*, and his writing provides helpful insights into all three texts. Although dealing with quite complex ideas, Carroll's clarity and organisation make this an excellent book for those who want to think through some of the issues involved in the interrelations between art, literature, culture and politics. It also helpfully places Lyotard's thought in relation with other contemporary French critical thinkers.

Diacritics volume 14 number 3 (Fall 1984)

This is a special issue of the journal, *Diacritics*, devoted to Lyotard's work. It contains a series of extremely useful reviews of Lyotard's texts by a number of writers whose work on Lyotard has been exemplary, including David Carroll, Georges Van Den Abeele, Bill Readings and Geoffrey Bennington. There is also a brief interview with Lyotard about his career up to the publication of *The Differend*.

Hutchings, Kimberly (1996) *Kant, Critique and Politics*, London: Routledge.

This book provides a clear introduction to Kant's critical philos-ophy, and some helpful discussions of the ways in which it has been taken up by more recent thinkers such as Habermas and Lyotard. The section that deals explicitly with Lyotard provides insightful discussions of *The Postmodern Condition*, *Just Gaming* and *The Differend*, as well as his essays on history. Lyotard's, sometimes problematic, reading of Kant is explained with care and attention. This is a good introduction to the important differences between contemporary interpretations of Kantian philosophy and politics, and a helpful analysis of one of Lyotard's key philosophical sources.

Readings, Bill (1991) *Introducing Lyotard: Art and Politics*, London: Routledge.

A very good introduction to the whole range of Lyotard's philosophy that, although quite difficult in places, uses a range of illustrations from culture to demonstrate the potential impact of such key notions as the sublime, the differend and the event. Readings' extensive use of examples drawn from art, culture and history make this an engaging and helpful book about Lyotard's political philoso-phies of art and culture.

Sim, Stuart (1996) *Jean-François Lyotard*, Hemel Hempstead: Prentice Hall and Harvester Wheatsheaf.

This is one of the most straightforward introductions to Lyotard's work, and makes an excellent next step for students wanting to find out more about the movement from his early Algerian writings to his postmodern philosophy. Sim clearly maps out the development of Lyotard's work, and provides some important insights about his postmodern theory and its relation to Marxism.

Sim, Stuart (2001) *Lyotard and the Inhuman*, Cambridge: Icon Books.

This is a very short and accessibly written book that investigates recent challenges to humanist philosophy. Although it draws quite heavily on Lyotard's arguments in *The Inhuman*, it also provides helpful introductions to other thinkers who write about the blurring of boundaries between humans and cyborgs and the 'computerisation' of our society.

Williams, James (1998) *Lyotard: Towards a Postmodern Philosophy*, Cambridge: Polity Press.

This introduction traces Lyotard's thought from his early writings up to *The Inhuman*, and provides clear and independently minded readings of most of the key texts. Williams reads Lyotard from the perspective of Nietzsche rather than Kant, which gives his analyses quite a different inflection from those contained in this book. The clarity of the writing makes this a helpful text, and the final section on debates in which Lyotard has been involved is insightful and usefully sets his work in the context of recent philosophical and political discussions.

Williams, James (2000) *Lyotard and the Political*, London: Routledge.

This is quite a complex book, and one that challenges the value of some of Lyotard's more recent postmodern arguments. Most useful, perhaps, is the analysis of his early writings on Algeria and his break with Marxism. Moreover, the discussions of *Libidinal Economy*, which Williams sees as Lyotard's most important book, are extremely clear, detailed and raise important issues for contemporary thought.

WORKS CITED

Armstrong, Isobel (2000) *The Radical Aesthetic*, Oxford: Blackwell.

Badmington, Neil (ed.) (2000), *Posthumanism*, Basingstoke: Palgrave.

Baudrillard, Jean (1994) *The Illusion of the End*, trans. Chris Turner, Cambridge: Polity.

—— (1995) *The Gulf War Did Not Take Place*, trans. Paul Patton, Sydney: Power.

Benjamin, Andrew (ed.) (1992) *Judging Lyotard*, London: Routledge.

Bennington, Geoffrey (1988) *Lyotard: Writing the Event*, Manchester: Manchester University Press.

Brewster, Scott, Joughlin, John, Owen, David and Walker, Richard (eds) (2000) *Inhuman Reflections: Thinking the Limits of the Human*, Manchester: Manchester University Press.

Browning, Gary (2000) *Lyotard and the End of Grand Narratives*, Cardiff: University of Wales Press.

Carroll, David (1987) *Paraesthetics: Foucault, Lyotard, Derrida*, London: Methuen.

Davis, Tony (1997) *Humanism*, London: Routledge.

Eagleton, Terry (1990) *The Ideology of the Aesthetic*, Oxford: Blackwell.

—— (1996) *The Illusions of Postmodernism*, Oxford: Blackwell.

Elam, Diane (1992) *Romancing the Postmodern*, London: Routledge.

Farquhar, George (1973) *The Recruiting Officer*, London: Davis-Poynter.

Freud, Sigmund (1953) *The Interpretation of Dreams*, trans. James Strachey, Harmondsworth: Penguin.

Gelder, Ken and Jacobs, Jane M. (1998) *Uncanny Australia: Sacredness and Identity in a Postcolonial Nation*, Victoria: Melbourne University Press.

Habermas, Jürgen (1987) *The Philosophical Discourse of Modernity: Twelve Lectures*, trans. Frederick Lawrence, Cambridge: Polity.

Harrison, Charles and Wood, Paul (1992) *Art in Theory 1900–1990: An Anthology of Changing Ideas*, Oxford: Blackwell.

Harvey, David (1990) *The Condition of Postmodernity*, Oxford: Blackwell.

Hegel, G. W. F. (1969) *Science of Logic*, trans. A. V. Miller, London: George Allen & Unwin.

—— (1970) *Hegel's Philosophy of Nature: Part Two of the Encyclopedia of the Philosophical Sciences*, trans. W. Wallace and A. V. Miller, Oxford: Oxford University Press.

—— (1971) *Hegel's Philosophy of Mind: Part Three of the Encyclopedia of the Philosophical Sciences*, trans. W. Wallace and A. V. Miller, Oxford: Oxford University Press.

—— (1975a) *Hegel's Logic: Part One of the Encyclopedia of the Philosophical Sciences*, 3rd edn, trans. W. Wallace, Oxford: Oxford University Press.

—— (1975b) *Aesthetics: Lectures on Fine Art*, trans. T. M. Knox, Oxford: Clarendon Press.

—— (1977) *Hegel's Phenomenology of Spirit*, trans. A. V. Miller, Oxford: Oxford University Press.

Hutcheon, Linda (1988) *A Poetics of Postmodernism*, London: Routledge.

—— (1989) *The Politics of Postmodernism*, London: Routledge.

Hutchings, Kimberly (1996) *Kant, Critique and Politics*, London: Routledge.

Jameson, Fredric (1981) *The Political Unconscious: Narrative as a Socially Symbolic Act*, London and New York: Routledge.

—— (1991) *Postmodernism, or, The Cultural Logic of Late Capitalism*, London: Verso.

Jardine, Alice (1985) *Gynesis: Configurations of Woman and Modernity*, Ithaca and London: Cornell University Press.

Jenkins, Keith (1999) *Why History? Ethics and Postmodernity*, London: Routledge.

Kant, Immanuel (1929) *Critique of Pure Reason*, trans. Norman Kemp Smith, London: Macmillan.

—— (1963) *On History*, Lewis White Beck (ed.), Indianapolis: Bobbs-Merrill.

—— (1987) *Critique of Judgement*, trans. Werner S. Pluhar, Indianapolis and Cambridge: Hackett.

—— (1993) *Critique of Practical Reason*, trans. Lewis White Beck, New York and Basingstoke: Macmillan.

Klein, Melanie (2000) *No Logo*, London: Flamingo.

Librett, Jeffrey S., trans. (1993) *Of the Sublime: Presence in Question*, Albany: State University of New York Press.

Lyotard, Jean-François (1984) *The Postmodern Condition: A Report on Knowledge*, trans. Geoff Bennington and Brian Massumi, Manchester: Manchester University Press.

—— with Jean-Loup Thébaud (1985) *Just Gaming*, trans. Wlad Godzich, Minneapolis: University of Minnesota Press.

—— (1988a) *The Differend: Phrases in Dispute*, trans. Georges Van Den Abeele, Manchester: Manchester University Press.

—— (1988b) *Peregrinations: Law, Form, Event*, New York: Columbia University Press.

—— (1989) *The Lyotard Reader*, Andrew Benjamin (ed.), Oxford: Blackwell.

—— (1990a) *Heidegger and 'the jews'*, trans. Andreas Michael and Mark Roberts, Minneapolis: University of Minnesota Press.

—— (1990b) *Duchamp's TRANS/formers*, Venice, California: Lapis Press.

—— (1991a) *The Inhuman: Reflections on Time*, trans. Geoffrey Bennington and Rachel Bowlby, Cambridge: Polity Press.

—— (1991b) *Phenomenology*, trans. B. Bleakley, Albany, New York: State University of New York Press.

—— (1992) *The Postmodern Explained: Correspondence 1982–1985*, trans. Don Barry, Bernadette Maher, Julian Pefanis, Virginia Spate and Morgan Thomas, Minneapolis: University of Minnesota Press.

—— (1993a) *Libidinal Economy*, trans. Iain Hamilton Grant, London: Athlone.

—— (1993b) *Toward the Postmodern*, eds. Robert Harvey and Mark S. Roberts, New Jersey: Humanities Press.

—— (1993c) *Political Writings*, trans. Bill Hutchings and Kevin Paul Geiman, London: University College London Press.

—— (1994) *Lessons on the Analytic of the Sublime*, trans. Elizabeth Rottenberg, Stanford, California: Stanford University Press.

—— (1997) *Postmodern Fables*, trans. Georges Van Den Abeele, Minneapolis: University of Minnesota Press.

—— (1998) *The Assassination of Experience by Painting – Monory*, trans. Rachel Bowlby, London: Black Dog.

—— with Eberhard Gruber (1999a) *The Hyphen: Between Judaism and Christianity*, trans. Pascale-Anne Brault and Michael Nass, New York: Humanity Books.

—— (1999b) *Signed, Malraux*, trans. Robert Harvey, Minneapolis: University of Minnesota Press.

—— (2000) *The Confession of Augustine*, trans. Richard Beardsworth, Stanford, California: Stanford University Press.

—— (2001) *Soundproof Room: Malraux's Anti-Aesthetics*, trans. Robert Harvey, Stanford: California: Stanford University Press.

Monbiot, George (2000) *Captive State: the Corporate Takeover of Britain*, Basingstoke: Macmillan.

Norris, Christopher (1990) *What's Wrong With Postmodernism*, Hemel Hempstead: Harvester Wheatsheaf.

Orwell, George (1983) *The Complete Novels*, Harmondsworth: Penguin.

Passerin D'Entrèves, Maurizio and Benhabib, Seyla (eds) (1996) *Habermas and the Unfinished Project of Modernity*, Cambridge: Polity.

Readings, Bill (1991) *Introducing Lyotard: Art and Politics*, London: Routledge.

Rushdie, Salman (1981) *Midnight's Children*, London: Cape.

Sim, Stuart (1996) *Jean-François Lyotard*, Hemel Hempstead: Prentice Hall and Harvester Wheatsheaf.

—— (2001) *Lyotard and the Inhuman*, Cambridge: Icon Books.

Wertenbaker, Timberlake (1996) *Plays One*, London: Faber and Faber.

Williams, James (1998) *Lyotard: Towards a Postmodern Philosophy*, Cambridge: Polity.

—— (2000) *Lyotard and the Political*, London: Routledge.

Wittgenstein, Ludwig (1967) *Philosophical Investigations*, trans. G. E. M. Anscombe, Oxford: Blackwell.

—— (1974) *Tractatus Logico-Philosophicus*, trans. D. F. Pears and B. F. McGuinness, Oxford: Blackwell.

INDEX